CLIMATE CHANGE KITCHEN

FIGHT GLOBAL WARMING WITH GOOD FOOD

Mathew Hampshire-Waugh

Crowstone Publishing

First Published 2023

By Crowstone Publishing

www.crowstonepublishing.com

Copyright © 2023 Mathew Hampshire-Waugh

All rights reserved. No part of this book may be reprinted or reproduced or utilized in any form or by any electronic, mechanical, or other means, now known or hereafter invented, including photocopying and recording, or in any information storage or retrieval system, without permission in writing from the publishers.

Trademark notice: Product or corporate names may be trademarks or registered trademarks and are used only for identification and explanation without intent to infringe.

Originally published by Crowstone Publishing in 2023. Crowstone Publishing is a trading name of Net-Zero Consulting Services Ltd whose address can be found at www.net-zero.consulting.

British Library Cataloguing-in-Publication Data

A catalogue record for this book is available from the British Library.

ISBN: 978-1-9989975-2-7

TABLE OF CONTENTS

CREATING THE CLIMATE KITCHEN 6

GOOD FOR YOU 7

GOOD FOR THE PLANET 8

CLIMATE KITCHEN HACKS 10

MEASUREMENTS & EQUIPMENT 13

EASY EATS & SHARING PLATES 14
- Loaded nachos with cashew melt 14
- Pulled pork & jackfruit sliders 16
- Pecan veggie rolls 18
- Quesadillas with sweet potato melt 20
- Yakitori chicken skewers 22

SIMPLE STARTERS & SIDES 24
- Baby bruschetta 24
- Parmesan croquettes 26
- Mini tuna fishcakes 28
- Lean chicken koftas 30
- Wholesome beetroot frittata 32
- Gobi manchurian cauliflower 34

DELIGHTFUL DIPS 36
- Cashew hummus 36
- Garden pea guacamole 38
- Tangy tzatziki 40
- Baba ghanoush 42

SUPER SOUPS 44
- Creamy chicken & cauliflower broth 44
- Zingy gazpacho soup 46
- Tangy shellfish tom yum 48
- Luscious laksa 50
- Hearty harira soup 52

SENSATIONAL SALADS 54
Chicken caesar salad 54
Minted greek salad 56
Beetroot niçoise salad 58
Waldorf salad 60
Avocado caprese salad 62
Spicy thai tuna salad 64
Sweet papaya thai salad 66

COMFORT FOODS 68
Not-fried chicken burgers 68
Ham-burger & fries 70
Three cheese mac & cheese 72
Piri piri chicken & corn cutlets 74
Smoky chicken fajitas 76
Spicy bean burritos 78
Light & crispy tonkatsu pork 80

PERFECT PASTAS 82
Pork bolognese 82
Classic pasta carbonara 84
Summer veggie lasagna 86
Tuna pasta bake with a parmesan crunch 88
Pasta puttanesca 90
Pasta alla norma 92

WINTER WARMERS 94
Smoky pork chili 94
Crispy crumb cassoulet 96
Chicken, leek, and sweet potato pie 98
Aromatic vegetable tagine 100
Lighter moussaka 102

CLASSIC CURRIES 104
Chicken tikka masala 104
Korma curry 106
Cauliflower & coconut jalfrezi 108
Japanese curry rice 110
Crispy aubergine katsu curry 112
Chicken rendang curry 114
Veggie thai red curry 116
Bunny chow 118

FAKE-AWAYS 120
Shiitake chow mein 120
Kung pao chicken 122
Lean sweet & sour chicken...124
Scallop pad thai 126
Chicken gyros...128
Yakisoba chicken 130

SOUL BOWLS 132
Easy scallop risotto 132
Simple seafood paella..134
Smoky mackerel kedgeree 136
Chicken biryani 138
Crispy pork ramen bowl..140
Bibimbap 142

THE SCIENCE BIT..144

INDEX...148

CREATING THE CLIMATE KITCHEN

If you had told me twenty or even two years ago that I was going to write a cookbook I wouldn't have believed you. My career started out in science, where I earned a doctorate in chemistry researching ways to improve solar panels, before spending ten years working on electric cars and renewable energy at a global investment bank.

I always held a deep interest in climate so in 2019 I decided to take the plunge. I quit my job and spent three years researching and writing a non-fiction book on all aspects of global warming. My book 'CLIMATE CHANGE and the road to NET-ZERO' shows that a rapid transition to a low-carbon system is not only best for the planet but also the economy. Since publishing the book, I have been working hard to share that message with investors, companies, and environmental groups.

I can now see a clear path to net-zero through new technologies across many of our global systems. But agriculture is very different. Reaching net-zero food will rely more heavily on cultural change in our everyday food choices and eating habits.

"I began to ask myself, is it possible to continue to celebrate the world's favorite recipes whilst also protecting the planet?

This question became the inspiration for the Climate Change Kitchen. The idea, to combine my experience in chemistry and finance with my love of cooking - to crunch the numbers, carbon-hack classic recipes, and re-imagine the world's favorite dishes for a low-carbon future.

The Climate Change Kitchen recipes have, on average, a 75% lower carbon footprint, 20% fewer calories, and 40% less fat with the same serving size and amazing taste. Cook each of the 65 recipes in this book once (instead of the traditional recipes) and you will avoid half a tonne of green-house gas emissions.

GOOD FOR YOU AND GOOD FOR THE PLANET

GOOD FOR YOU

Everyone knows that eating well is key to a healthy, happy lifestyle but making the correct food choices can often be confusing, especially when cooking at home. That's why all the recipes in the Climate Change Kitchen come with a calorie count and a breakdown of nutritional content. The recipes have also been 'hacked' not only to lower the carbon footprint, but also to reduce the calorie content and improve the balance of protein, carbohydrates, and fat. Helping you enjoy delicious meals which are good for you and good for the planet.

COUNTING CALORIES The recommended daily calorie (kcal) intake for your average healthy adult is 2,000 - 2,500 calories. This should include 6-8 glasses of water and at least 5 portions of fruit & veg per day. General advice is to eat less red or processed meat, smaller quantities of sugary treats, and to avoid saturated fat, whilst eating more beans & pulses and choosing unsaturated oils like olive or canola oil.

BALANCING NUTRIENTS Fat, protein, and carbohydrates are collectively known as macronutrients, the food sources that provide us with energy (calories). A healthy diet consists of a balanced intake of macronutrients with roughly 15% of calories from protein, 30% of calories from fat, and 55% of calories from carbohydrates.[1]

KEEPING COUNT Trying to eat healthy? The Climate Kitchen has got you. All our recipes provide a clear calorie count per serving, the balance of macro-nutrients as a percentage of calories, and labels on all recipes that qualify as: vegetarian, vegan, low calorie, low fat, low in saturated fat, low-carb, or high in protein. Helping you make more informed food choices with all your favorite recipes.

Label	Definitions
Low Calorie Main	Less than 500 kcal per main meal serving
Low Calorie Side	Less than 250 kcal per soup, side, or salad serving
Low Fat	Less than 20% of kcal from fat
Low in Saturated Fat*	Less than 5% of kcal from saturated fat
Low Carbohydrate	Less than 25% of kcal from carbohydrates
High Protein	More than 30% of kcal from protein

*To reduce the risk of heart disease saturated fat should account for less than 10% of calories and ideally towards 5% as given by Dietary Guidelines for Americans, USDA.

[1] Percentage values are based on the maximum and minimum values from the ranges given by *Dietary Guidelines for Americans,* USDA, 2020 & Government Dietary Recommendations, Public Health England, 2016. Low-Carbohydrate Diet, National Library of Medicine, Robert Oh et al, 2023.

GOOD FOR THE PLANET

Agriculture is responsible for one quarter of all global greenhouse gas emissions. Half of agricultural emissions come from the carbon dioxide released when forests are cut down to make way for expanding agricultural land. The other half from excess fertilizer use, cow and sheep burps, and the burning of fossil fuels for farm equipment, refrigeration, and transport.

To avoid the worst impacts of climate change agriculture must reach net-zero by the middle of this century. We must eliminate ongoing agricultural emissions and reverse the expansion of farmland.

Some of the required changes (such as improving production yields, reducing supply chain waste, and low carbon farming techniques) must be driven by governments and the farming industry. But individual changes will also play a large role in decarbonizing agriculture through our everyday eating choices:

FOOD CHOICES

The type of ingredients you eat have the biggest impact on the carbon footprint of the food system. Food choices influence the emissions from land-use, farming, and food processing which together account for 70% of the carbon footprint of our food.

- **Meat products** have the highest carbon footprint owing to the large area of land needed to rear animals. In fact, two thirds of all agricultural land is used for animal grazing and just one third is used for growing crops (half of which are then fed to animals). Yet, despite the meat industry using nearly one quarter of dryland on planet Earth, meat provides just 20% of our daily calorie intake.

- **Beef and lamb** have the highest carbon footprint of all foods because cows and sheep have a unique way of digesting food that releases large quantities of methane - a particularly potent greenhouse gas. The methane from cows and sheep alone accounts for 5% of all global greenhouse gas emissions - that's nearly as much as deforestation.

- **Seafood emissions** come from the diesel burnt to power the boats, destruction of the ocean floor during bottom trawling, and in processing and transporting the fish. Always opt for locally-sourced, sustainably certified fish caught by handline, pole and line, or troll fishing where possible.

- **Plant-based products** have the lowest carbon footprint - grains, rice, vegetables, and fruit require less land, less processing, and create less waste. Field-grown, seasonal, locally sourced plant-based products have the lowest footprint of all.

COOKING CHOICES

Food waste and the energy used during cooking accounts for 20% of the carbon footprint of food. Reducing waste, particularly in the higher emissions ingredients, is very important. Reducing food waste also ties into the importance of portion control for a healthy lifestyle. The way you cook food generally has a smaller impact on carbon emissions but moving away from natural gas and towards electric cooking equipment supports decarbonization efforts and eliminates the harmful air pollutants released into your kitchen from burning natural gas.

BUYING CHOICES

It may come as a surprise but the transportation, refrigeration, and packaging of food account for just 10% of the total carbon footprint. Buying locally sourced, seasonal produce with sustainable packaging helps support efforts to decarbonize the food system - but don't forget it's the type of food we eat which has a far bigger impact on fighting climate change.

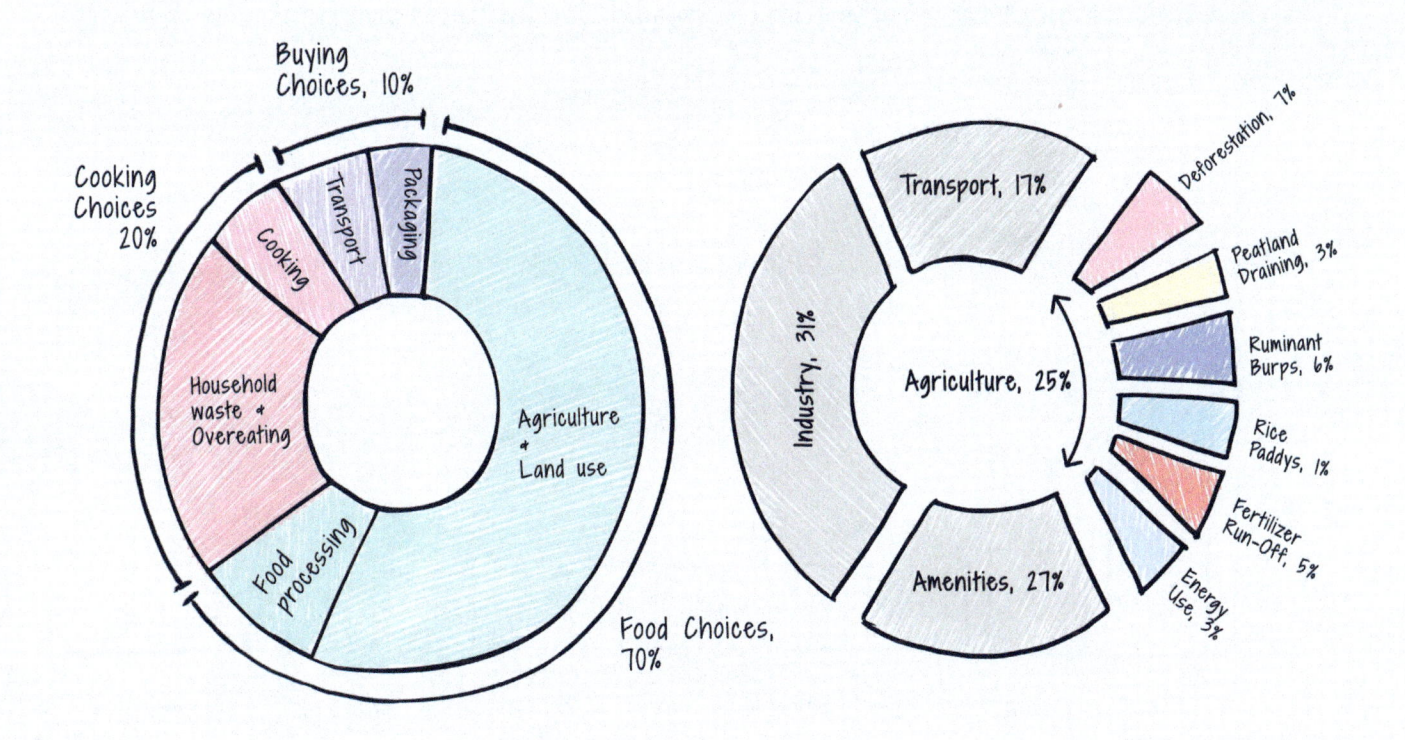

The Carbon Footprint of Food

- Buying Choices, 10% (Transport, Packaging)
- Cooking Choices 20% (Cooking, Household waste & Overeating)
- Food Choices, 70% (Food processing, Agriculture & Land use)

Data Source: Based on lifecycle emissions given by the 'The Big Climate Database', Version 1, Concito, 2021 using aggregated emissions by category from 90 of the most popular home cooked dishes from around the world.

Global Greenhouse Gas Emissions

- Transport, 17%
- Industry, 31%
- Amenities, 27%
- Agriculture, 25% (Deforestation, 7%; Peatland Draining, 3%; Ruminant Burps, 6%; Rice Paddys, 1%; Fertilizer Run-Off, 5%; Energy Use, 3%)

Data Source: Climate Change and the road to Net Zero, Crowstone Publishing, Mathew Hampshire-Waugh, 2021.

CLIMATE KITCHEN HACKS

Each of the classic recipes in the Climate Change Kitchen has been 'hacked' to lower the carbon footprint, reduce the calorie count, and improve the balance of protein, carbohydrates, and fat. Our simple labelling system makes cooking great tasting, healthy and sustainable food super easy. Here are some of the key principles which guide us at the Climate Change Kitchen:

800 IS THE MAGIC NUMBER Each of our main meal servings is less than 800 calories with a carbon footprint of less than 800 grams[3]. Why? Well, 800 calories is around the maximum recommended calorie count for the main meal of the day for a healthy adult. And 800 grams of carbon dioxide (CO_2) is less than half the average carbon footprint of a main meal today. If you combine this small but crucial change with bigger systems changes and reforestation, you are supporting a pathway to net-zero agriculture (starters, soups, and salads are all less than 400 calories & 400 grams of CO_2 per serving).

EAT YOUR GREENS, GREEN YOUR EATS Switching from meat to plant-based ingredients is a sure-fire way to lower the carbon footprint and lower the calorie count of a dish. By using high-protein, plant-based ingredients you can create great tasting, nutritionally balanced and low carbon versions of your favorite meals. Jack fruit, sweet potato, beans, pulses, avocados, peas, and nuts are great substitutes, with a lower carbon footprint and packed with flavor.

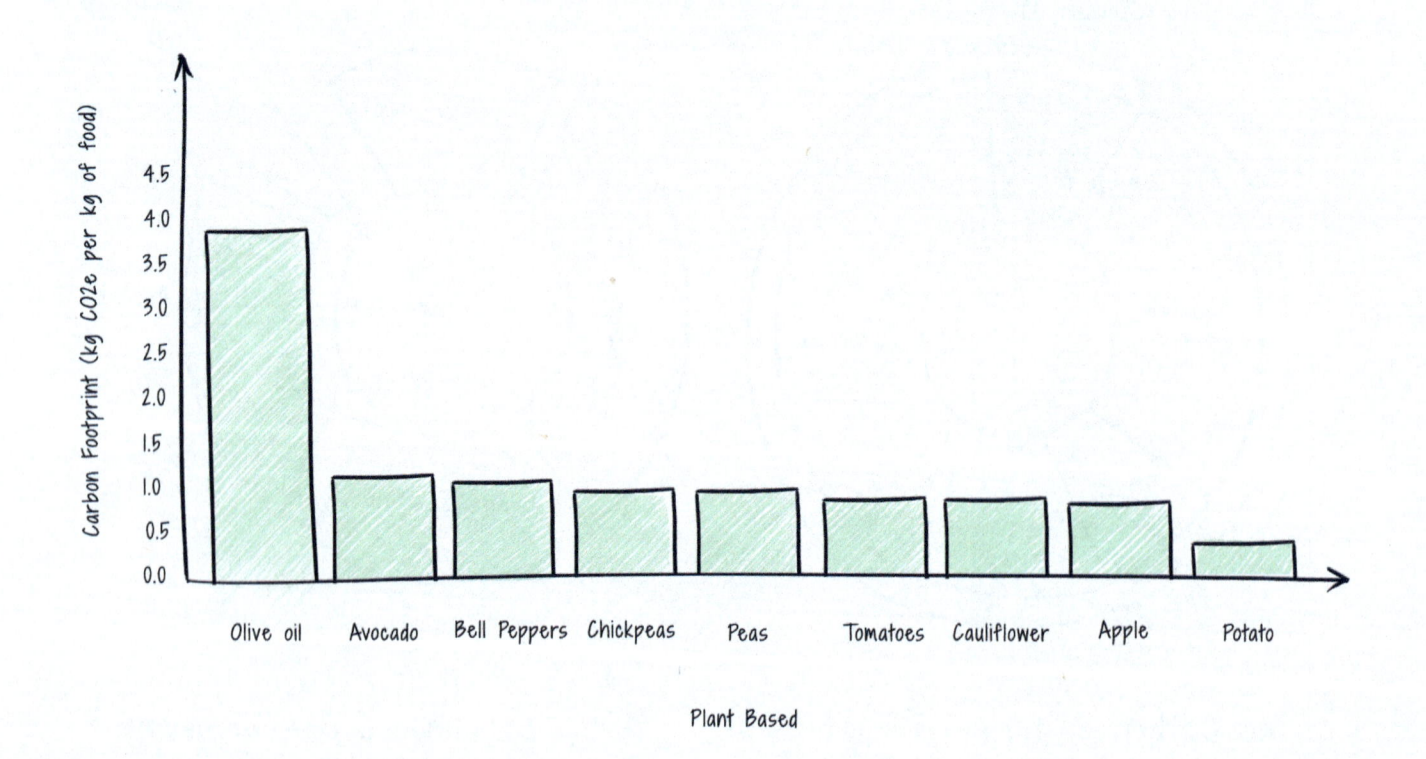

Carbon Footprint (kg CO2e per kg of food) — Plant Based: Olive oil, Avocado, Bell Peppers, Chickpeas, Peas, Tomatoes, Cauliflower, Apple, Potato

---

[3] This is 800 grams of carbon dioxide equivalents CO_2e which includes carbon dioxide, methane, nitrous oxide and other greenhouse gas emissions measured on a comparable basis.

CHOICE MEATS, MEAT CHOICES Here at the Climate Change Kitchen we get it – you still want to enjoy cooking and eating meat. We've got your back. By making smart meat choices you can dramatically lower the carbon footprint of your favorite dishes and improve nutritional balance. Switching out beef, lamb, or goat and replacing them with pork, chicken or seafood can reduce the carbon footprint of the meal by more than half. Avoiding red meats also means less of the stuff that's bad for you; cholesterol, saturated fat, and high sodium. The Climate Kitchen recipes combine smart meat choices and simple flavor hacks to enhance the taste, texture, and visual appeal of your favorite meals.

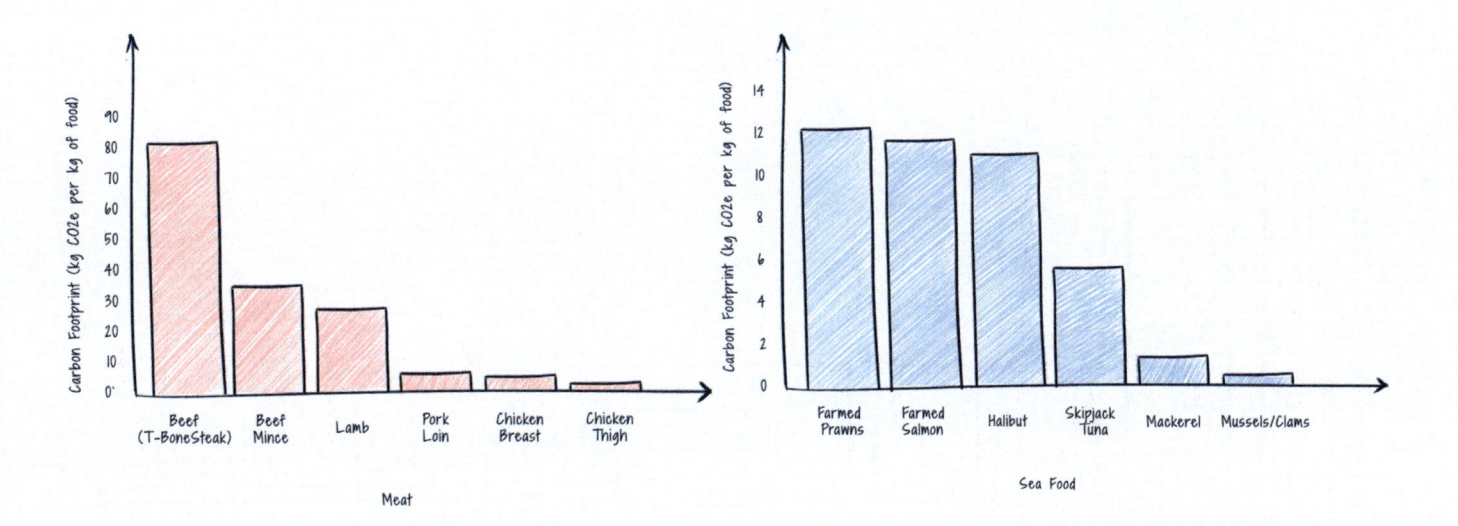

PLENTY OF FISH IN THE SEA? Our recipes favor the lowest footprint seafoods which include mollusks such as clams, mussels, or scallops, farmed on the coastline where they help to filter the water and can actually improve the aquatic environment. We avoid crustaceans such as prawns or lobsters, because over half of these products are farmed at the expense of natural mangroves, and most of the remainder are caught at sea using harmful trawling techniques. For fish, we favor line caught species that gather in large schools, - anchovies, sardines, mackerel and skipjack tuna - making them easy to catch and with the lowest carbon footprint. Wild-caught white fish and salmon are okay-ish. We avoid farmed fish (aquaculture) or trawl caught fish which risk a higher carbon footprint.

SPRAY DON'T DRIZZLE Oils are an essential part of cooking; they help to raise the cooking temperature, prevent ingredients sticking to the pan, and impart flavor in the cooking process. But did you know that just four tablespoons of oil have nearly 500 calories and a carbon footprint of more than 200 grams of CO_2. We like to spray our oil because replacing each tablespoon with just 4 sprays of oil you can reduce the calories and carbon emissions by 75%. We favor olive oil with its healthy fat content for low temperature recipes or dressings, and for higher temperature cooking we use canola (rapeseed) oil which has a higher smoking point and avoids the formation of potentially harmful chemical compounds.

DOS AND DON'TS OF DAIRY The cow is no longer king. There are an abundance of dairy alternatives out there which, if chosen well, can add great taste, texture, and nutrition to your cooking. Try using oat or soy milk in place of coconut milk or single cream to add that silky texture with less fat and a lower carbon footprint. Use soy-based yogurt in place of crème fraiche or sour cream, avoiding that dairy. Natural yogurt is better than Greek yogurt as it uses one quarter of the milk to produce. But if you love Greek don't fret - soft cheeses like Feta have half the emissions of hard cheese options. If using hard cheese use sparingly as a flavor enhancer rather than main ingredient.

Bar chart: Carbon Footprint (kg CO2e per kg of food)

Category	Item	Approx. value
Cheese	Parmesan	~7.5
Cheese	Monterey Jack	~7.5
Cheese	Feta	~3
Milk & Yogurt	Greek Yogurt	~3
Milk & Yogurt	Cream	~2
Milk & Yogurt	Plain Yogurt	~1.3
Milk & Yogurt	Milk	~0.7
Milk & Yogurt	Oat Milk	~0.4
Milk & Yogurt	Soy Milk	~0.4

USE IT DON'T LOSE IT We try to create all our recipes using standard portions of perishable ingredients. This helps to minimize the number of half empty packets, and half used vegetables cluttering your fridge, going bad, and ending up in the trash.

SMASH IT, DON'T TRASH IT Cooking isn't always easy. At the climate kitchen we understand - which is why we have developed simple to follow, foolproof recipes you will get right first time and every-time - meaning no wasted food! We include simple tips like adding big flavors little by little (think lemon, garlic, chili); choosing cooking temperatures carefully to avoid burning food; using appropriate pans because heavy pans reach higher heats and are great for searing meat, but lighter pans will better distribute heat and help to avoid burning more delicate ingredients; or cooking stir fry ingredients in batches knowing that home woks often can't maintain the same high temperatures as commercial versions.

Carbon Footprint Data Sources: "CONCITO (2021): The Big Climate Database, version 1" - or subsequent versions & the "Seafood Carbon Emissions Tool", Dalhousie University & Monterey Bay Aquarium Seafood Watch®

MEASUREMENTS & EQUIPMENT

MEASUREMENTS
Life can be hard enough already, so to make it easier we provide measurements in both imperial and metric, by volume and weight, and using both US and European conventions. We specify if ingredients are dry, wet, or drained weight.

1 cup = 240 milliliter (ml)   1 tablespoon (tbsp) = 15 ml   1 teaspoon (tsp) = 5 ml

EQUIPMENT
The one piece of equipment we recommend you buy is an oil sprayer (they cost as little as a few dollars, pounds, or euros). Oil sprayers create an even, well distributed mist which means you can use far less oil in the cooking process. Each spray is about 1 ml of oil and 4 sprays replace 1 tbsp of drizzled oil.

You can often buy oil which is prefilled in a spray bottle, but it's cheaper to buy a couple of oil sprayers and fill from regular oil bottles. We use one for canola (rapeseed) oil and one for olive oil. If you don't have an oil sprayer don't worry, you can drizzle the oil as usual until you get around to buying one.

Should you require food processors, blenders, wire racks, or specific dish sizes for a recipe we will list the equipment at the bottom of the ingredients to make sure you don't get caught out mid-way through cooking.

COOKING TEMPERATURES
With Fahrenheit (°F), degree Celsius (°C) and gas marks, oven temperatures are confusing and difficult to convert. To make life easier we provide all three options for each recipe. We favor cooking with a fan-assisted (convection) oven, so the main temperatures are given accordingly. However, if you have a non-fan (conventional) oven we also provide adjusted temperatures. Always ensure you preheat your oven, and it has achieved the desired temperature before starting to cook.

SOURCING INGREDIENTS
We recommend using good quality, fresh ingredients but we also know that everyone has a budget so frozen, vac packed, or freeze-dried is fine by us. Just ensure the ingredients are de-frosted or rehydrated and ready to use. The one ingredient where we highly recommend spending a little more time or money on is the stock or broth. Homemade stock/broth or readymade from the shop are ideal, gel pots that you mix up are okay, but please avoid stock powders or cubes which are often too salty or synthetic tasting and can ruin a dish.

LOADED NACHOS WITH CASHEW MELT

EACH SERVING

350g	300	13%	34%	53%
CARBON	CALORIES	PROTEIN	FAT	CARBS

BALANCED MACRONUTRIENTS • VEGETARIAN

Serves 8 (snack portion)   Prep Time: 10 mins   Cooking Time: 10 mins

---

LOADED NACHOS were invented in Mexico in 1943 by a maître d' named Ignacio "Nacho" Anaya who rustled up a quick meal for guests that had arrived after the kitchen closed. This recipe is our take on Nachos' nachos and we think he would approve. Our loaded nachos are smothered in sumptuous sweet potato and cashew nut melt, salty olives, and if you can handle the heat... fiery jalapeños.

CLIMATE KITCHEN HACKS we replace some of the high carbon footprint cheese with a low carbon sweet potato & cashew nut melt. We switch hard cheese for mozzarella to give a better melt and less saturated fat, nicely complimented by a good dollop of reduced fat sour cream. The same serving size has a 45% lower carbon footprint, 25% fewer calories, and 50% less fat than standard loaded nachos recipes.

Easy Eats & Sharing Plates

INGREDIENTS

- 2 sweet potatoes (300g), whole
- 2 bags (14oz/400g) of tortilla chips
- 1 ball (125g) mozzarella cheese, shredded
- 1-2 tomatoes (1 cup, 240g), diced
- 1/4 cup (60g) red onion, finely diced
- 1/4 cup (60g) black olives, sliced
- 1/4 cup (60g) jalapeño peppers (optional), sliced
- 1/2 cup (60g) cashews (fairtrade certified)
- 1 cup (240 ml) vegetable broth
- 1/2 cup (120g) reduced fat sour cream
- 1/2 cup (120g) guacamole (try the Climate Kitchen recipe in dips section)
- 2 tbsp chopped fresh cilantro/coriander
- Food processor or hand blender

INSTRUCTIONS

1. Prick the sweet potato with a fork and microwave (at 800W power) for 6-9 minutes until soft.
2. Preheat your fan assisted oven to 320ºF / 160ºC / Gas mark 3 (for a non-fan oven 350ºF / 180ºC / Gas mark 4).
3. Assemble, measure, and prepare the ingredients.
4. Spread a layer of tortilla chips on a non-stick baking sheet (or baking sheet lined with parchment paper). Sprinkle the shredded mozzarella cheese on top of the tortilla chips. Add the diced tomatoes, red onion, black olives, and jalapeño pepper.
5. Bake for 8-10 minutes or until the cheese is melted and the nachos are heated through.
6. Meanwhile, place the soft insides of the cooked sweet potato in a blender/hand blender and add the cashews and vegetable broth. Pulse until smooth with a firm yogurt-like consistency. You may need to shake or stir the mix as it blends to help it along (don't be tempted to add more liquid as this will make the melt too runny).
7. Remove the nachos from the oven and top with the sweet potato melt, sour cream, guacamole and fresh cilantro/coriander.

PULLED PORK & JACKFRUIT SLIDERS

EACH SERVING

400g	400	25%	25%	50%
CARBON	CALORIES	PROTEIN	FAT	CARBS

Serves 8 (snack portion)　　Prep Time: 30 mins　　Cooking Time: 4 Hours

---

SLIDERS got their name in the US Navy canteens of the 1940s, who would serve up mini beef burgers so greasy the sailors said they would slide down in just one bite. Our sliders are far from greasy; they are filled with tangy rich pork, melt in the mouth jackfruit, and crunchy fresh slaw. The perfect balance of sweet and savory.

CLIMATE KITCHEN HACKS we switch out the beef from traditional slider recipes and replace it with pulled pork and jackfruit to reduce the carbon footprint whilst supercharging the plant-based goodness. You can also eliminate the mayo from the slaw because the pulled pork is so deliciously moist. The same serving size has an 80% lower carbon footprint, 10% fewer calories, and 30% less fat than your average beef slider recipe.

Easy Eats & Sharing Plates

INGREDIENTS

For the pulled pork:
- 1 can of young green jackfruit (400g, 200g drained)
- 1 cup (240ml) chicken broth/stock
- 2 tbsp (30ml) white wine vinegar
- 1/2 cup (120g) ketchup
- 1 tbsp apple sauce
- 2 tbsp light brown sugar
- 1 tbsp Worcestershire sauce
- 1 tsp paprika
- 1 tsp garlic powder
- 1/2 tsp cayenne chili pepper
- A pinch of pepper
- 1 lb (500g) small pork loin
- 12 slider buns

For the No-Mayo Slaw:
- 1/2 head small green cabbage (400g), very finely shredded
- 1/2 cup (120g) carrots, very finely shredded
- 1 small apple, very finely shredded
- 2-3 spring/green onions (50g, ½ cup), sliced length ways
- 1 tbsp (15ml) white wine vinegar
- 1 tsp (5ml) mustard
- 2 tbsp olive oil
- Salt and pepper, to taste

INSTRUCTIONS

1. Assemble, measure, and prepare the ingredients.
2. Preheat your fan assisted oven to 300°F / 150°C / Gas mark 2 (for a non-fan oven 325°F / 170°C / Gas mark 3).
3. Drain and rinse the jackfruit in cold water. Place the jackfruit inside soft kitchen paper or an old tea-towel and gently bash with a rolling pin - this will break-up the tougher parts of the jack fruit whilst also partly drying the fruit and allowing it to absorb all the delicious flavors from the sauce.
4. In a bowl, mix the broth/stock, vinegar, ketchup, apple sauce, brown sugar, Worcestershire sauce, paprika, garlic powder, cayenne pepper, and pepper.
5. Place the pork shoulder and drained/rinsed jackfruit in a baking dish (we find a loaf tray works really well because it fills up high to keep the pork tender) and pour the marinade over it. Cover the dish with foil and bake in the preheated oven for 3-4 hours, or until the pork is tender and falling apart.
6. Meanwhile mix the shredded cabbage, carrot, spring onion, and apple in a bowl with the vinegar, mustard, and olive oil. Season with salt and pepper to taste. Cover and leave in the refrigerator whilst the pork is cooking to let the vinegar soften the vegetables.
7. Remove the pork/jackfruit from the oven and let it cool for a few minutes. Transfer the meat and jackfruit to a bowl and, using two forks, shred the pork and jackfruit, discarding any fat or bones. Spoon the sauce from the roasting tray over the top of the shredded pork to add extra moisture and flavor - but make sure you don't leave the pork so wet it soaks through the bread buns.
8. Heat a large skillet over medium heat and place the slider buns, cut side down, in the skillet. Cook until the buns are toasted.
9. Assemble the sliders by placing a generous amount of pulled pork on the bottom half of each bun. Top with the no-mayo slaw and place the other half of the bun on top.

PECAN VEGGIE ROLLS

EACH SERVING

270g	400	6%	44%	50%
CARBON	CALORIES	PROTEIN	FAT	CARBS

VEGETARIAN

Serves 6 (side dish portion) | Prep Time: 20 mins | Cooking Time: 30 mins

---

PECAN VEGGIE ROLLS, deliciously rich and flaky pastry balanced by the fresh bite of carrots and zucchini and a satisfying crunch of rich pecans. Once you try our veggie rolls you won't go back.

CLIMATE KITCHEN HACKS we replace the pork sausage meat with plant-based fillings. We spray don't drizzle the oil when pan frying. And we use chopped pecans in the filling to add a rich taste and texture. The same serving size has a 60% lower carbon footprint, 30% fewer calories, and 30% less fat than regular pork sausage roll recipes.

INGREDIENTS

- 8 sprays canola (rapeseed) oil
- 1 medium onion (1/2 cup, 120g), finely diced
- 1 cup (100g) mushrooms, diced
- 2 cloves of garlic, minced/crushed
- 4-5 carrots (1 cup, 240g), grated
- 1 zucchini/courgette (1 cup, 240g), grated
- 1/4 cup (40g) breadcrumbs
- 1/2 cup (50g) pecans, finely chopped
- 1 tsp dried thyme
- 1/2 tsp mustard powder
- Salt and pepper, to taste
- 1 large sheet puff pastry (about 11oz/320g)
- 1 egg, beaten (for egg wash)

Dipping Sauce (optional)
- 3 tbsp mayo
- 2 tsp English mustard

INSTRUCTIONS

1. Assemble, measure, and prepare the ingredients.
2. Preheat your fan assisted oven to 400°F / 200°C / Gas mark 6 (for a non-fan oven 425°F / 220°C / Gas mark 7).
3. In a large skillet, heat 4 sprays of olive oil over a medium-high heat. Add the onion and mushrooms, fry until softened, about 3-4 minutes, add the garlic for a further 30 seconds.
4. Add another 4 sprays of oil and stir in the grated carrots, grated zucchini/courgette, breadcrumbs, chopped pecans, thyme, mustard powder, and a pinch of salt and pepper. Cook for an additional 5 minutes.
5. Roll out the puff pastry on a lightly floured surface to a rectangle about 12x16 inches / 30x40 cm.
6. Once the vegetable mixture has cooled, spoon the filling in a line (1-2 inch / 2.5-5cm wide), about 2 inches / 5cm from the shorter edge of the rectangular pastry. Fold and roll the exposed pastry edge over the filling (trim away any excess pastry this will create 2 further rolls) and seal the edges of the roll by dabbing egg wash to glue the pastry together. Use the back of a fork to press the two pastry edges firmly together.
7. Repeat the process with the remaining filling and pastry. From the one large pastry sheet you should end up with 3 large rolls (12 inches / 30cm long).
8. Finally, cut the rolls into 1-inch / 2.5cm slices. Place the slices on a baking sheet lined with parchment paper (pastry side up). Brush the remaining beaten egg over the top of the pastry rolls.
9. Bake for 18-25 minutes or until golden brown.
10. Whilst the veggie rolls are cooking, mix the mayo and English mustard in a small dish to create your dipping sauce. Remove the sausage rolls from the oven. Let them cool for a few minutes before serving warm with the mustard mayo.

QUESADILLAS WITH SWEET POTATO MELT

EACH SERVING

400g	400	15%	45%	40%
CARBON	CALORIES	PROTEIN	FAT	CARBS

Serves 4 (snack portion) · Prep Time: 15 mins · Cooking Time: 15 mins

QUESADILLA literally means "cheesy little thing". This recipe takes the humble quesadilla to the next level with crispy griddled tortillas packed full of chicken, cheese, and peppers, served up with our creamy cashew melt. These Mexican parcels of goodness are a firm favorite.

CLIMATE KITCHEN HACKS we replace the large quantities of cheese in traditional recipes with creamy avocado and a delicious cashew melt to reduce the carbon footprint and reduce the saturated fat content. The same serving size has a 50% lower carbon footprint, 25% fewer calories, and 40% less fat than regular quesadilla recipes.

20 Easy Eats & Sharing Plates

INGREDIENTS

- 1 large sweet potato (150g), whole
- 4-8 sprays of canola (rapeseed) oil
- 4 flour tortillas
- 1/2 cup (120g) red bell pepper, finely diced
- 1/4 cup (60g) cooked chicken, shredded
- 1/2 cup (120g) avocado, sliced
- 1/2 cup (120g) shredded cheese (cheddar, Monterey Jack, or a blend)
- 1/4 cup (30g) cashews (fairtrade certified)
- 1/2 cup (120 ml) vegetable broth
- Food processor or hand blender

INSTRUCTIONS

1. Prick the sweet potato with a fork and microwave (at 800W power) for 6-9 minutes until soft.
2. Preheat a fan-assisted oven to 175°F / 80°C / Gas mark 1 (for a non-fan oven 210°F / 100°C / Gas mark 1).
3. Assemble, measure, and prepare the ingredients.
4. Heat a skillet over a low-medium heat. Coat the pan with 1-2 sprays of oil.
5. Place a tortilla in the skillet and sprinkle over a layer of diced pepper, chicken, avocado and cheese to cover the whole tortilla base.
6. Using a spatula, fold the tortilla over to form a half-moon shape. Cook until the cheese is melted and the tortilla is golden brown, about 2-3 minutes per side.
7. Repeat with the remaining tortillas and filling. Keeping the cooked tortillas warm in the oven.
8. While the tortillas are cooking, place the soft inside of the cooked sweet potato, cashews, and vegetable broth in a blender and pulse until smooth. The mix should have a firm yogurt-like consistency. You may need to shake or stir the mix as it blends (don't be tempted to add more liquid as this will make the melt too runny).
9. Cut each of the cooked quesadillas into wedges.
10. Serve hot with the sweet potato and cashew melt dip and a wedge of lime.

YAKITORI CHICKEN SKEWERS

EACH SERVING

240g	310	40%	35%	25%
CARBON	CALORIES	PROTEIN	FAT	CARBS

HIGH PROTEIN

- Serves 4 (side dish portion)
- Marinate Time: 30 mins
- Prep Time: 10 mins
- Cooking Time: 15 mins

YAKITORI means "grilled bird" and these tasty skewers are a quintessential Japanese street food. The skewers are made by marinating bite-size pieces of chicken in a sweet soy glaze and grilling to perfection. Perfect for parties or BBQs. The recipe uses chicken thighs which have a low carbon footprint for meat.

Easy Eats & Sharing Plates

INGREDIENTS

- 4 tbsp soy sauce
- 3 tbsp mirin
- 2 tbsp brown sugar
- 2 cloves of garlic, minced/crushed
- 1 tsp grated ginger
- 1 lb (450g) boneless, skinless chicken thighs, cut into 1-inch/2.5 cm cubes
- 8-10 skewers (if using wooden skewers, soak them in water for at least 30 minutes before using)
- 1 tbsp sesame seeds, to serve
- 1-2 green/spring onion, sliced, to serve
- Dipping sauce, to serve (optional)

INSTRUCTIONS

1. Assemble, measure, and prepare the ingredients.
2. In a small bowl, mix the soy sauce, mirin, brown sugar, garlic, and ginger.
3. Thread the chicken onto skewers, leaving a little space between each piece.
4. Place the skewers in a shallow dish and pour the marinade over them, making sure each skewer is well coated. Cover and marinate in the refrigerator for at least 30 minutes (or up to overnight).
5. Once ready to cook the skewers, preheat your grill to a medium-high heat.
6. Grill the skewers for 10-15 minutes, turning as each side browns, until the chicken is cooked through and the glaze is caramelized. If using wooden skewers, you may need to cover the exposed wooden ends with aluminum foil to prevent burning.
7. Once cooked, remove the skewers from the grill and serve immediately with a sprinkle of sesame seeds, green/spring onion slices, and your favorite dipping sauce.

BABY BRUSCHETTA

EACH SERVING

140g	175	11%	28%	61%
CARBON	CALORIES	PROTEIN	FAT	CARBS

BALANCED MACRONUTRIENTS • LOW IN SATURATED FAT
VEGAN OPTION • LOW CALORIE

Serves 4 (side dish portion)   Prep Time: 10 mins   Cooking Time: 20 mins

BRUSCHETTA was created by Italian peasant farmers who would rub tomatoes into slices of bread as a quick snack. The recipe is now a classic Italian appetizer with crispy bread, sweet tomatoes, and tangy onion. Our mini bruschetta may be small in size but they pack a big flavor.

CLIMATE KITCHEN HACKS we use an oil sprayer to coat the baguette without over saturating it. We avoid cheese and instead add flavor with balsamic vinegar. This recipe is great for using up baguette that has started to go stale. The same serving size has a 35% lower carbon footprint, 40% fewer calories, and 70% less fat compared to regular bruschetta recipes.

Simple Starters & Sides

INGREDIENTS

- 2 cloves of garlic, whole
- 1 small baguette (about 10 inches or 25cm), cut into 1/2-inch (1.25 cm) slices (vegan option)
- 16 sprays of olive oil
- 2 cups (480g) diced tomatoes (a mix of cherry tomatoes and vine ripened work great)
- 1/4 cup (60g) red onion, finely diced
- 1/4 cup chopped basil
- 2 tsp balsamic vinegar
- Salt and pepper, to taste

INSTRUCTIONS

1. Assemble, measure, and prepare the ingredients.
2. Preheat your oven to 320°F / 160°C / Gas mark 3 (for a non-fan oven 350°F / 180°C / Gas mark 4)
3. Heat the unpeeled garlic clove in a skillet/pan on a medium-high heat for 5 minutes to deactivate the enzyme that causes the very intense garlic hit and aftertaste. Remove from the skillet/pan and mince/crush.
4. Spray the olive oil over both sides of the sliced baguette. Mix the crushed garlic with a couple of sprays of oil and spread the garlic oil over the top of the sliced baguette with a pastry brush or the back of a spoon.
5. Place the slices on a baking sheet and bake for 8-10 minutes, or until golden brown.
6. Meanwhile in a medium bowl, mix the diced tomatoes, red onion, chopped basil, balsamic, salt, and pepper. After the mix has been sitting for 5 minutes the tomatoes may have released their juices so you may wish to strain away the excess juice using a sieve (to avoid soggy bruschetta).
7. Once the bread is done toasting, remove it from the oven, let it cool, and top each slice with a healthy spoonful of the tomato mixture.

PARMESAN CROQUETTES

EACH SERVING

210g	390	14%	23%	63%
CARBON	CALORIES	PROTEIN	FAT	CARBS

BALANCED MACRONUTRIENTS • VEGETARIAN

Serves 4 (side dish portion) Prep Time: 30 mins Cooking Time: 10 mins

---

CROQUETTE comes from the French word 'croquer' which means to crunch, munch or nibble. Our potato-based take on this French classic has a super crispy outside and a melt in the mouth middle; perfect for crunching, munching, and nibbling.

CLIMATE KITCHEN HACKS we make our croquettes from potato rather than flour because potatoes have two thirds lower calorie content and carbon footprint. We use strong tasting cheese to maximize flavor without adding too much saturated fat. We spray the cooking oil rather than deep or shallow frying and use golden breadcrumbs to absorb less oil whilst still creating that crispy exterior. The same serving size has a 30% lower carbon footprint, 40% fewer calories, and 50% less fat than regular croquette recipes.

Simple Starters & Sides

INGREDIENTS

- 2 large potatoes (2 cups, 450g), peeled and roughly cubed
- 1 cup (100g) grated Parmesan (or Gruyere)
- 1 egg, beaten
- 2 tbsp (30g) all-purpose flour
- 1/2 cup (50g) dry golden breadcrumbs
- 1 tsp paprika
- 16 sprays of canola (rapeseed) oil for frying

INSTRUCTIONS

1. Assemble, measure, and prepare the ingredients.
2. Boil the potatoes for 20 minutes until soft. Drain and mash.
3. In a large bowl, mix the mashed potatoes and grated cheese.
4. Shape the mixture into 12 small oblong shapes (having 4 flat sides makes the frying easier and requires less oil).
5. Place the beaten egg in one shallow dish and the flour in another. Place mixed breadcrumbs and paprika in another shallow dish. Roll the croquettes in flour, then dip them in the beaten egg and finally roll in the breadcrumbs.
6. Heat a non-stick pan with a couple of sprays of oil and fry the croquettes for 2-3 minutes on each side until crispy. As you turn the croquettes spray the pan with a little extra oil to ensure a hot frying surface.
7. The croquettes are best served warm straight from the pan. Delicious.

MINI TUNA FISHCAKES

EACH SERVING

390g	400	36%	18%	46%
CARBON	CALORIES	PROTEIN	FAT	CARBS

HIGH PROTEIN • LOW FAT • LOW IN SATURATED FAT

Serves 4 (side dish portion)   Prep Time: 30 mins   Cooking Time: 15 mins

MINI TUNA FISH CAKES pack a delicious and healthy protein hit. Melt in the mouth texture, flavorful, and high in protein whilst low in saturated fat. They make a great sharing plate or appetizer.

CLIMATE KITCHEN HACKS we use line caught skipjack tuna in place of the traditional white fish. Skipjack tuna are plentiful and easy to catch providing a sustainable source of fish with a lower carbon footprint. Go easy on the oil by using a sprayer and the same serving size has a 50% lower carbon footprint and 35% less fat than standard fish cake recipes.

INGREDIENTS

- 1-2 large potatoes (240g), whole
- 3 cans (300g in total, drained weight) skipjack tuna in brine (handline, pole-and-line, or troll caught)
- 1/2 cup (60g) onion, diced
- 2 cloves of garlic, minced/crushed
- 2 tbsp chopped fresh parsley
- 1 tsp mustard (Dijon works well)
- 1 tsp lemon juice
- Salt and pepper, to taste
- 1/2 cup (60g) all-purpose flour
- 2 eggs
- 1 cup (100g) breadcrumbs
- 8 sprays canola (rapeseed) oil for frying

INSTRUCTIONS

1. Assemble, measure, and prepare the ingredients.
2. Microwave the potatoes whole for 7-9 minutes (800W power) until soft in the middle. Once cool enough to handle, scoop out the soft inside.
3. In a large bowl, combine the tuna, potato inside, onion, garlic, parsley, mustard, lemon juice, and a good pinch of salt & pepper. Mix well.
4. Form the mixture into 16 mini cakes (roughly the size of your inner palm).
5. Place the flour, eggs, and breadcrumbs each in three separate shallow dishes.
6. Dredge each fish cake in the flour, then dip into the egg, and finally coat in the breadcrumbs.
7. Heat a large skillet over medium-high heat and spray enough oil to cover the bottom of the pan.
8. Carefully place the fish cakes in the hot pan, gentle press down to ensure good contact with the pan, and cook for 3-4 minutes per side or until golden brown and cooked through (use more oil if required).
9. Remove the fish cakes from the pan. Serve the fish cakes immediately with your favorite dipping sauce (vegan mayo mixed with sweet chili goes great).

LEAN CHICKEN KOFTAS

EACH SERVING

290g	300	41%	40%	19%
CARBON	CALORIES	PROTEIN	FAT	CARBS

HIGH PROTEIN • LOW CARB

Serves 4 (side dish portion)   Prep Time: 10 mins   Cooking Time: 10 mins

---

KOFTA recipes date back over 800 years; little middle eastern meatballs packed full of flavorful spices and garlic. Our mini koftas are great for party snacks or as a delicious starter dish. Quick, easy, and a guaranteed hit.

CLIMATE KITCHEN HACKS we switch the traditional lamb meat for leaner chicken or turkey mince and go easy on the oil to reduce the carbon footprint and lower the saturated fat. The same serving size has a 90% lower carbon footprint, 10% fewer calories, and 30% less fat than regular lamb kofta recipes.

Simple Starters & Sides

INGREDIENTS

- 1lb (450g) ground/minced chicken or turkey
- 1/4 cup (60g) onion, finely diced
- 2 cloves of garlic, minced/crushed
- 1/2 cup (60g) breadcrumbs
- 2 tbsp chopped cilantro/coriander
- 2 tbsp chopped parsley
- 1 tsp ground cumin
- 1 tsp ground coriander
- 1/2 tsp ground cinnamon
- Salt and pepper, to taste
- 4 sprays canola (rapeseed) oil for frying

INSTRUCTIONS

1. Assemble, measure, and prepare the ingredients. Make sure to dice the onion very finely so the koftas hold together during cooking.
2. In a large bowl, mix the ground/minced chicken, diced onion, garlic, breadcrumbs, cilantro/coriander, parsley, cumin, coriander, cinnamon, salt, and pepper.
3. Mix well until all the ingredients are evenly distributed.
4. Shape the mixture into oblong shapes (they are easier to flip and cook with flat sides).
5. Heat a large griddle pan or skillet over a medium heat or preheat your grill to a medium-high temperature. Add the koftas to the skillet or grill, spray coat with oil, and cook for about 8-10 minutes, turning occasionally, until golden brown on each side and cooked through.
6. Remove the koftas from the skillet or grill and dry the excess oil on a kitchen paper lined plate.
7. Serve the koftas with your favorite dipping sauce (our low carbon Tzatziki goes beautifully).

WHOLESOME BEETROOT FRITTATA

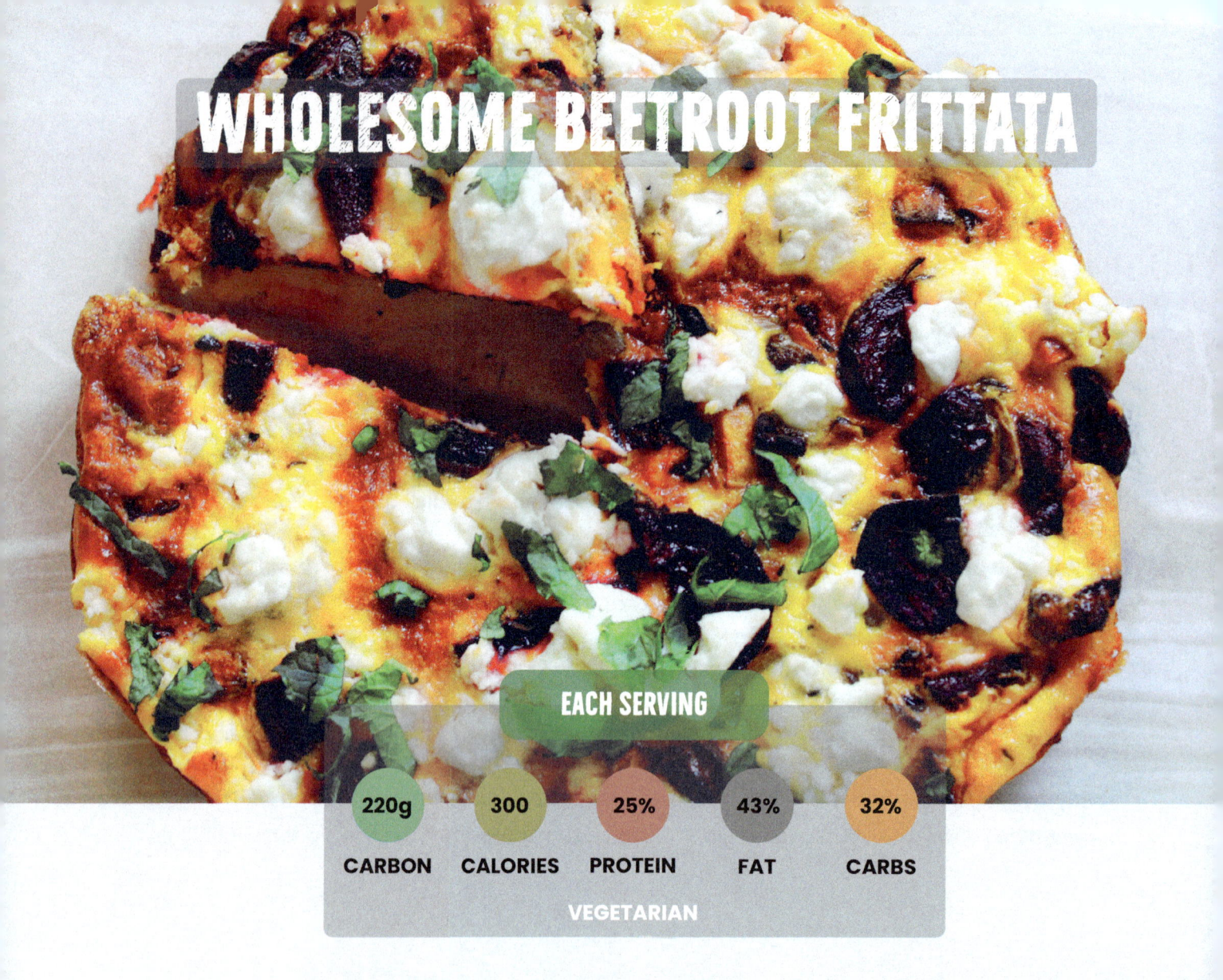

EACH SERVING

220g	300	25%	43%	32%
CARBON	CALORIES	PROTEIN	FAT	CARBS

VEGETARIAN

Serves 4 (side dish portion)   Prep Time: 10 mins   Cooking Time: 30 mins

---

FRITTATA, an Italian classic similar to an omelette. Deliciously simple, but packed with flavor; vibrant, earthy fresh beetroot balanced by sumptuous sweet potato and salty Feta cheese - a perfect weeknight sharing dish.

CLIMATE KITCHEN HACKS we replace the usual grated cheese with a semi-soft feta - soft cheeses use as little as half the milk in production and also require less aging; that means they generate less than half the carbon emissions of semi-hard cheeses like cheddar or Monterey Jack. The same serving size has a 50% lower carbon footprint, 10% fewer calories, and 35% less fat than comparable hard cheese veggie frittata recipes.

INGREDIENTS

- 2 medium sweet potatoes (1 cup, 240g), peeled and diced (½ inch / 1.5cm)
- 1 cup (240g) raw beet(root), diced (½ inch / 1.5cm)
- 1 small onion (1/2 cup, 120g), diced (½ inch / 1.5cm)
- 6 sprays of canola (rapeseed) oil
- 1/2 tsp dried thyme
- 6 eggs
- 1/4 cup (60ml) whole milk
- Salt and pepper
- 1/4 cup (60g) feta cheese
- 1 tbsp fresh mint leaves, chopped

INSTRUCTIONS

1. Preheat the oven to 400°F / 200°C / Gas mark 6 (for a non-fan oven 425°F / 220°C / Gas mark 7).
2. Assemble, measure, and prepare the ingredients.
3. Place the sweet potato, beetroot, and onion on a baking tray. Spray 4 sprays of oil, sprinkle over the thyme to coat, and roast in the oven for 20-25 mins, until the vegetables start to caramelize on the edges.
4. Meanwhile in a large bowl, whisk together the eggs, milk, and a pinch of salt and pepper.
5. Heat a skillet on a low-medium heat with a few sprays of oil. Add the roasted vegetables then pour over the egg mixture and cook for about 5-7 minutes or until the bottom is set (use a low-medium heat to avoid the bottom burning). Note: If you do burn the bottom of the frittata don't worry as you can always trim the bottom off before serving.
6. Crumble on the feta cheese and put the skillet under the broiler/grill for 2-3 minutes or until the top is golden brown and set. Remove from the broiler/grill, let it cool, sprinkle over the mint and serve.

GOBI MANCHURIAN CAULIFLOWER

EACH SERVING

200g	230	11%	37%	52%
CARBON	CALORIES	PROTEIN	FAT	CARBS

LOW IN SATURATED FAT • BALANCED MACRONUTRIENTS • LOW CALORIE • VEGAN

Serves 6 (side dish portion) | Prep Time: 20 mins | Cooking Time: 20 mins

GOBI MANCHURIAN is a popular Indian-Chinese dish of deep-fried cauliflower tossed in a sweet, spicy and tangy sauce first created by Chinese chef, Nelson Wang, at the Cricket Club of India in 1975. Our version cuts back on the oil, creating a super healthy, super tasty, plant-based super food which is great for sharing plates, platters, or as a side dish.

CLIMATE KITCHEN HACKS by roasting rather than deep frying the cauliflower you can enjoy a sharing plate with a very low carbon footprint, which has a perfect balance of macro-nutrients, is low in saturated fat, vegan, and of course delicious - it ticks all the boxes! The same serving size has a 20% lower carbon footprint, 50% fewer calories, and 70% less fat than the traditional deep-fried recipes.

Simple Starters & Sides

INGREDIENTS

- 2 tbsp all-purpose flour
- 1/4 tsp salt
- 1/4 tsp black pepper
- 1/2 tsp mild red chili powder
- 1 head cauliflower (1kg), cut into florets
- 8 sprays canola (rapeseed) oil
- 1 small onion (1/2 cup, 75g), finely diced
- 2 tsp fresh ginger, finely sliced or grated
- 1/2 tsp garlic powder
- 1 red bell pepper (1 cup 150g), diced
- 1 tomato (1/2 cup, 60g), diced
- 2 tbsp soy sauce
- 1 tsp red chili sauce/siracha
- 1 tbsp tomato ketchup
- 1/4 tsp black pepper
- 1/2 tsp sugar
- Salt to taste
- 2 tbsp chopped cilantro/coriander, to garnish

INSTRUCTIONS

1. Preheat a fan assisted oven to 375ºF / 190ºC / Gas mark 5 (for a non-fan oven 410ºF / 210ºC / Gas mark 6).
2. Assemble, measure, and prepare the ingredients.
3. In a bowl, mix the flour, salt, black pepper, and red chili powder. Sprinkle the mix over the cauliflower florets and transfer to a roasting tray.
4. Spray the cauliflower florets with 4 sprays of oil to coat and roast in the oven for 20-25 minutes, halfway through cooking spray extra oil and toss the cauliflower to ensure they turn an even golden-brown color.
5. As the cauliflower cooks, spray 2 sprays of oil to coat a large saucepan and add the onion for 2-3 minutes until softened, add the ginger for another 1-2 minutes, finally add the garlic powder, bell pepper, and tomato. Cook for 3-4 minutes, until the vegetables are tender, spray extra oil during cooking if needed.
6. Add soy sauce, red chili sauce, tomato ketchup, black pepper, sugar, and a pinch of salt to the pan. Stir well and bring to the boil.
7. Add the roasted cauliflower florets to the sauce and toss until well coated.
8. Garnish with chopped cilantro/coriander and serve hot.

CASHEW HUMMUS

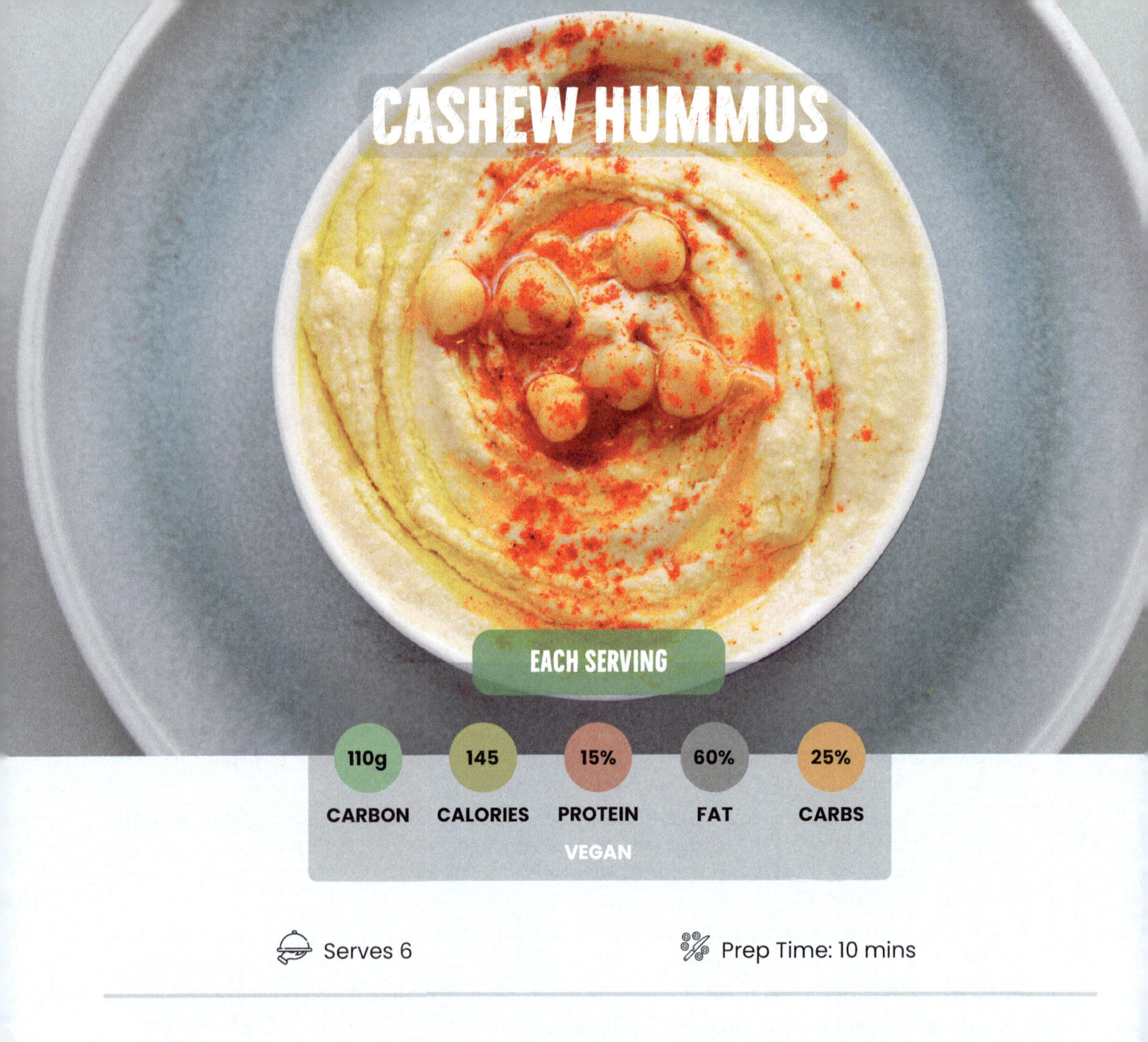

EACH SERVING

110g	145	15%	60%	25%
CARBON	CALORIES	PROTEIN	FAT	CARBS

VEGAN

Serves 6 Prep Time: 10 mins

HUMMUS is short for hummus bi tahina which literally means "chickpeas with tahini" in Arabic. It is a traditional middle eastern dip that is great for serving with flatbread, vegetables, or to accompany your favorite dish.

CLIMATE KITCHEN HACKS we reduce the oil content of our hummus and add a tablespoon of cashew butter. This creates a delicious nutty undertone whilst maintaining the creamy taste and velvety texture. It also means less fat and a lower carbon footprint. Nuts are a healthy source of protein with a relatively low carbon footprint, especially nuts that grow on trees. The same serving size has a 10% lower carbon footprint, 20% fewer calories, and 35% less fat than traditional hummus recipes.

Delightful Dips

INGREDIENTS

- 1 clove of garlic, whole
- 1 can/15 oz (225g, drained weight) chickpeas, drained and rinsed
- 1/4 cup (60ml) tahini
- 2 tbsp fresh lemon juice (30ml, 1 small lemon)
- 1 tbsp olive oilsp cashew butter (fairtrade certified)
- 1/2 cup (120ml) cold water
- Salt and pepper, to taste
- Paprika for garnish
- Food processor or hand blender

INSTRUCTIONS

1. Assemble, measure, and prepare the ingredients.
2. Heat the unpeeled garlic clove in a pan/skillet on a medium-high heat for 5 minutes to deactivate the enzyme that causes the very intense garlic hit and aftertaste. Remove from the skillet and mince/crush.
3. Next, in a food processor or blender, combine the chickpeas, tahini, half the lemon juice, minced garlic, olive oil, cashew butter, a pinch of salt & pepper, and half the water.
4. Blend until smooth and creamy, adding more water to get the desired texture (if using a food processor, you may need to carefully push the mixture around using a wooden spoon to help the blending - be careful of the blades!).
5. Taste, adjust salt and pepper as required, and add more lemon juice if needed. Transfer the hummus to a bowl, create a well in the center using a spoon. Drizzle some olive oil into the well and sprinkle with paprika.

GARDEN PEA GUACAMOLE

EACH SERVING

110g	100	10%	55%	35%
CARBON	CALORIES	PROTEIN	FAT	CARBS

VEGAN

Serves 6 Prep Time: 15 mins

GUACAMOLE is a creamy dip made from avocados and tomatoes, first made by the Aztecs who called it 'ahuaca-molli' meaning avocado-mashed. We super charge our guacamole recipe with garden peas for a fresh and vibrant take on this Mexican staple.

CLIMATE KITCHEN HACKS we reduce the avocado content by blending in garden peas to increase protein and reduce the fat content. The same serving size has a similar carbon footprint, but 20% fewer calories and 40% less fat than traditional guacamole.

Delightful Dips

INGREDIENTS

- 1 clove of garlic, minced/crushed
- 2 medium avocados (280g), ripe
- 1 can or 1 cup (180g) canned/frozen garden peas, ready to eat
- 1/4 cup (60g) cherry tomatoes cut into six
- 2 tbsp finely diced red onion
- 2 tbsp chopped fresh cilantro/coriander
- 1 tbsp fresh lime juice (15ml, 1 small lime)
- Salt and pepper, to taste

INSTRUCTIONS

1. Assemble, measure, and prepare the ingredients.
2. Heat the unpeeled garlic clove in a pan/skillet on a medium-high heat for 5 minutes to deactivate the enzyme that causes the very intense garlic hit and aftertaste. Remove from the skillet and mince/crush.
3. Cut the avocados in half and remove the pit.
4. Scoop the avocado flesh into a bowl. Add the drained garden peas.
5. Mash the avocado and peas with a fork or a potato masher to desired consistency.
6. Add the diced tomatoes, onions, cilantro/coriander, half the lime juice, and garlic.
7. Mix well. We love this guacamole chunky but you can blend it if you prefer a smoother consistency.
8. Add salt and pepper to taste, and more lime juice if needed.
9. Serve with tortilla chips, or use as a topping on tacos, burritos, and sandwiches.

TANGY TZATZIKI

EACH SERVING

90g	80	25%	40%	35%
CARBON	CALORIES	PROTEIN	FAT	CARBS

VEGETARIAN

Serves 6　　　　　　　　　　　　　　Prep Time: 10 mins

TZATSIKI is a traditional Greek dip made from yogurt, cucumber, and garlic. Our version uses natural yogurt rather than Greek yogurt which creates a thinner pouring dip which is the ideal accompaniment for rich meat dishes.

CLIMATE KITCHEN HACKS we switch the traditional Greek yogurt for natural yogurt to lower the carbon footprint. Greek yogurt takes three to four times more milk to produce than natural yoghurt. The same serving size has a 65% lower carbon footprint.

Delightful Dips

INGREDIENTS

- 1 clove of garlic, whole
- 1 1/2 cup (360g) plain/natural yogurt
- 1/2 cup (120g) diced cucumber, diced
- 2 tbsp chopped fresh dill or mint (depending on the accompanying dish)
- 1 tbsp fresh lemon juice (15ml, 1 small lemon)
- 1 tsp runny honey
- Salt and pepper, to taste
- 1 tbsp olive oil for garnish

INSTRUCTIONS

1. Assemble, measure, and prepare the ingredients.
2. Heat the unpeeled garlic clove in a skillet on a medium-high heat for 5 minutes to deactivate the enzyme that causes the very intense garlic hit and aftertaste. Remove from the skillet and mince/crush.
3. Next, in a large bowl, mix the natural/plain yogurt, cucumber, garlic, dill/mint, half the lemon juice, honey, and salt & pepper.
4. Taste and adjust salt and pepper as required and add more lemon juice if needed.
5. Transfer the tzatziki to a bowl and create a well in the center using a spoon.
6. Drizzle some olive oil into the well and sprinkle extra dill/mint over the top of the tzatziki.

BABA GHANOUSH

EACH SERVING

100g	90	5%	65%	30%
CARBON	CALORIES	PROTEIN	FAT	CARBS

VEGAN

Serves 4　　　Prep Time: 15 mins　　　Cooking Time: 40 mins

BABA GHANOUSH is a Levantine dip made from eggplant/aubergine, olive oil and lemon. We add a little tahini which strictly speaking turns the dish from Baba Ghanoush to Moutabal. The dip goes well with salads, veggies, and flatbread.

CLIMATE KITCHEN HACKS we use less oil than most Baba Ghanoush recipes but replace some of the oil content with a small amount of flavorful tahini. This reduces the emissions and fat content whilst maintaining that silky smooth texture and rich taste. We add zucchini/courgette to the dish for extra flavor and a better nutritional balance. The same serving size has a 20% lower carbon footprint, 40% fewer calories, and 45% less fat than traditional Baba Ghanoush.

INGREDIENTS

- 1 large eggplant/aubergine (1 lb, 450g)
- 1 zucchini/courgette (200g)
- 4 sprays of canola (rapeseed) oil
- 1 clove of garlic, whole
- 1 tbsp tahini
- 1 tbsp fresh lemon juice (15ml, 1 small lemon)
- 1 tbsp (15ml) olive oil
- Salt and pepper, to taste
- Chopped parsley or mint for garnish (optional)
- Food processor or hand blender

INSTRUCTIONS

1. Assemble, measure, and prepare the ingredients.
2. Preheat a fan assisted oven to 375°F / 190°C / Gas mark 5 (for a non-fan oven 410°F / 210°C / Gas mark 6)
3. Cut the eggplant/aubergine and zucchini/courgette in half, spray with oil, and place on a baking sheet, cut sides down. Roast in the oven for 30 minutes or until the eggplant skin is charred and the flesh is soft.
4. Meanwhile, heat the unpeeled garlic clove in a skillet/pan on a medium-high heat for 5 minutes to deactivate the enzyme that causes the very intense garlic hit and aftertaste. Remove from the skillet/pan and mince/crush.
5. Once the eggplant and zucchini are roasted, allow to cool, scoop out the flesh and discard the skin and excess water.
6. In a food processor or blender, combine the eggplant/aubergine flesh, zucchini/courgette flesh, tahini, minced garlic, half the lemon juice, and olive oil. Add salt and pepper to taste. Blend until smooth and creamy (if using a blender you may need to carefully push the mixture into the middle using a wooden spoon to help the mixing process - be careful of the blades!).
7. Taste and adjust the seasoning or add extra lemon juice as needed.
8. Transfer the dip to a serving bowl and garnish with chopped parsley or mint.

CREAMY CHICKEN & CAULIFLOWER BROTH

EACH SERVING

290g	250	23%	18%	59%
CARBON	CALORIES	PROTEIN	FAT	CARBS

LOW IN SATURATED FAT • LOW FAT • LOW CALORIE

Serves: 6 (starter portion)   Prep Time: 15 mins   Cooking Time: 40 mins

CHICKEN SOUP is the ultimate comfort food, perfect for a cold winter day or when you're feeling under the weather. We have taken this chicken soup recipe to the next level with a creamy broth, sweet cauliflower, rich chicken and tangy undertones of celery and herbs... it won't disappoint.

CLIMATE KITCHEN HACKS we swap half the chicken for cauliflower to reduce the meat content whilst adding extra flavor, texture, and nutrition. We use oat or soy milk rather than coconut milk or cream to reduce the carbon footprint and saturated fat content. The same serving size has a 50% lower carbon footprint, 40% fewer calories, and 75% less fat than regular cream of chicken soup recipes.

Super Soups

INGREDIENTS

- 2 chicken breasts (1/2 lb, 225g)
- 2 cups (480ml) chicken broth/stock
- 1 cup (240ml) water
- 2 cups (480ml) oat or soy milk (your preference, oat is creamier)
- 1 medium onion (1/2 cup, 120g), finely diced
- 2 cloves garlic, minced/crushed
- 2-3 carrots (1 cup, 240g), peeled and diced
- 1 celery stick (1/4 cup, 60g), finely sliced
- 1 tsp dried thyme
- 1 cauliflower head (400g), cut into bite size florets
- 1 cup (160g) medium thickness egg noodles
- Salt and pepper, to taste
- 2 tbsp of coriander or parsley, chopped (to serve)

INSTRUCTIONS

1. Assemble, measure, and prepare the ingredients.
2. In a large pot, add the chicken breast, chicken broth, water, oat or soy milk, onion, garlic, carrots, celery, and thyme. Cover the pot and bring to a boil.
3. Once boiling, reduce the heat and leave the pan covered (to retain the liquid broth without thickening too much) and simmer for 25 minutes.
4. Once simmering is complete, remove the cooked chicken breasts from the pot. Skim any excess chicken fat from the top of the soup, then add the cauliflower florets.
5. Shred the chicken using 2 forks and add back to the soup pot. Add the egg noodles to the pot and simmer for another 5 minutes or until the noodles and cauliflower are cooked through.
6. Taste the broth and season with salt and pepper to taste (it is important to taste the soup first as ingredients like celery or readymade stocks can already have a strong salty taste).
7. Mix half the chopped coriander or parsley through the broth and serve in bowls with the remainder of the coriander or parsley sprinkled on top.

ZINGY GAZPACHO SOUP

EACH SERVING

310g	200	10%	30%	60%
CARBON	CALORIES	PROTEIN	FAT	CARBS

LOW IN SATURATED FAT • BALANCED MACRONUTRIENTS
LOW CALORIE • VEGAN OPTION

Serves: 6 (starter portion) | Prep Time: 15 mins | Cooking Time: 120 mins

---

GAZPACHO is a zingy, light, and refreshing Spanish soup. It is served chilled and perfect for a hot summer's day.

CLIMATE KITCHEN HACKS gazpacho is naturally low carbon footprint, low calorie and nutritionally well balanced so long as you go easy on the olive oil. Use a little less oil and the same serving size has a 5% lower carbon footprint, 15% fewer calories, and 40% less fat than regular gazpacho recipes.

INGREDIENTS

- 2 cloves garlic, whole and unpeeled
- 4 large tomatoes (2 cups, 480g), peeled, de-seeded and diced
- 1 large cucumber (2 cups, 300g), peeled & diced
- 1 red bell pepper (1 cup, 200g), deseeded & diced
- 1/2 red onion (1/2 cup, 100g), finely diced
- 2 cups (480ml) tomato juice
- 2 tbsp extra-virgin olive oil
- 2 tbsp red wine vinegar
- Salt and pepper, to taste
- 1/4 cup fresh basil or cilantro/coriander, chopped
- 1/2 cup (75g) croutons (vegan option)

INSTRUCTIONS

1. Heat the unpeeled garlic cloves in a skillet/pan on a medium-high heat for 5 minutes to deactivate the enzyme that causes the very intense garlic hit and aftertaste. Remove from the skillet/pan and mince/crush.
2. Meanwhile, assemble, measure, and prepare the ingredients. Take extra care preparing the vegetables - make sure to remove all the skin, seeds, and pith to create a super smooth, velvety gazpacho.
3. In a large bowl, combine the tomatoes, cucumber, bell pepper, onion, and garlic. Reserve 6 tbsp of the mix for garnish. Cover and refrigerate.
4. In a separate bowl, whisk together the tomato juice, olive oil, red wine vinegar, and a pinch of salt & pepper.
5. Pour the tomato juice mixture over the main bowl of vegetables and stir well. Add to a blender and blend to your desired consistency (if you like it even smoother you can strain with a sieve once well blended - use a tablespoon to push the gazpacho through).
6. Chill the gazpacho in the refrigerator for at least 2 hours.
7. Before serving, adjust the salt and pepper to taste.
8. Serve the gazpacho chilled, garnished with the reserved diced vegetables, cilantro/coriander or basil, croutons, and a drizzle of olive oil.
9. If you want to give it an extra kick you can add some cayenne pepper or chili oil.

TANGY SHELLFISH TOM YUM

EACH SERVING

170g	130	40%	20%	40%
CARBON	CALORIES	PROTEIN	FAT	CARBS

LOW IN SATURATED FAT • HIGH PROTEIN • LOW CALORIE

Serves: 6 (starter portion)   Prep Time: 10 mins   Cooking Time: 20 mins

TOM YUM soup is a tangy Thai dish that's super easy to make and packed with a bold flavors. This recipe perfectly balances the tangy, spiciness of the broth with the rich, saltiness of the mussels.

CLIMATE KITCHEN HACKS swap the traditional shrimp or prawns for mussels or clams to lower the carbon footprint of Tom Yum. Shrimp have a high carbon footprint due to the destruction of wetlands through aquaculture farming or through the destruction of the seabed by trawling at sea. Farmed mussels or clams are a far more sustainable addition that can actually filter and enhance our coastlines. The same serving size has an 80% lower carbon footprint than traditional shrimp based recipes.

Super Soups

INGREDIENTS

- 4 cups (1L) chicken or vegetable broth/stock
- 4 kaffir lime leaves
- 2 stalks of lemongrass, bruised (bash with a rolling pin)
- 1-3 bird's eye chilies (1 inch long chilis), deseeded and finely sliced
- 2 cloves of garlic, minced/crushed
- 2-3 shallots (1/2 cup, 100g), minced or very finely diced
- 2 cups (480g) of mussels or clams (sustainably farmed / fresh, vac-packed, or frozen)
- 2 cups (200g) baby bok choy, keep the smaller leaves whole and cut the large ones in half
- 1 1/2 tbsp fish sauce
- 1 tbsp fresh lime juice (15 ml, 1 small lime)
- 1 tbsp light brown sugar
- 1/4 cup chopped cilantro/coriander

INSTRUCTIONS

1. Assemble, measure, and prepare the ingredients. Be careful with the bird's eye chilies. One will give the dish a warm undertone, two will give a kick, three will start to make it fiery.
2. In a large pot, bring the chicken or vegetable broth/stock to a boil. Add the kaffir lime leaves, lemongrass, chilies, garlic, and shallots. Reduce the heat to medium-low and simmer for 10 minutes with the lid off to reduce/thicken the liquid slightly.
3. Meanwhile, prepare the clams or mussels per the instructions. If using fresh mussels/clams start by washing in salted cold water. Boil a pan of water, add the fresh mussels or clams, place the lid on firmly to make sure they steam for 5-10 minutes until they have all opened (discard any unopened clams or mussels).
4. Add the bok choy, fish sauce, lime juice, and brown sugar to the soup broth. Simmer for another 2-3 minutes. Remove from heat, stir in the cilantro/coriander and cooked mussels or clams.
5. Serve the Tom Yum Soup hot, garnishing with extra cilantro/coriander or chilies, if desired.

LUSCIOUS LAKSA

EACH SERVING

- **400g** CARBON
- **310** CALORIES
- **22%** PROTEIN
- **38%** FAT
- **40%** CARBS

Serves: 6 (starter portion) | Prep Time: 10 mins | Cooking Time: 15 mins

---

LAKSA is a deliciously spicy Southeast Asian dish that's perfect for noodle lovers! This recipe is easy to make and holds the perfect balance between the creamy, sweet & savory broth, the rich chicken, and crunchy fresh bite from the beansprouts.

CLIMATE KITCHEN HACKS we use chicken rather than prawns and swap half the coconut milk for oat or soy milk. The same serving size has a 50% lower carbon footprint, 10% fewer calories, and 30% less fat than traditional recipes.

INGREDIENTS

- 1 cup (240ml) coconut milk
- 1 cup (240ml) oat milk (or soy if preferred)
- 2 cups (480ml) chicken or vegetable broth/stock
- 2 red birds eye chili peppers, deseeded and finely chopped
- 2 lemongrass stalks, bruised (bash with a rolling pin)
- 2 kaffir lime leaves
- 2 garlic cloves, minced/crushed
- 2 shallots (1/2 cup, 50g), very finely diced
- 1 1/2 tbsp fish sauce
- 1 tbsp soy sauce
- 1/2 tbsp sugar
- 4 oz (110g, 2-3 nests) rice noodles
- 1 cup (240g) beansprouts
- 1 cup (240g) cooked chicken, shredded or sliced
- 2 tbsp chopped cilantro/coriander or basil, for serving
- 2 tbsp cashews, roughly chopped for serving
- Lime wedges, for serving

INSTRUCTIONS

1. Assemble, measure, and prepare the ingredients.
2. In a large pot, on a low-medium heat, warm the coconut milk, oat (or soy) milk, chicken or vegetable broth/stock, chili peppers, lemongrass, kaffir lime leaves, garlic, shallots, fish sauce, soy sauce and half the sugar. Gently simmer for 10 minutes (do not allow the soup to boil as the milk will separate). After 10 minutes taste and add more sugar if required (Laksa is a sweet tasting soup, sweeten to your preference).
3. Cook the rice noodles according to package instructions, then drain and rinse with cold water. If you prefer you can cut the noodles into smaller sections using scissors to make the soup easier to eat with a spoon.
4. Divide the noodles among 4 bowls. Strain the hot soup through a sieve to remove the onion then ladle the smooth soup over the noodles. Top each bowl with the beansprouts, shredded cooked chicken, cashews and cilantro/coriander or basil.
5. Serve the Laksa Soup hot, garnished with lime wedges.

HEARTY HARIRA SOUP

EACH SERVING

350g	300	28%	19%	53%
CARBON	CALORIES	PROTEIN	FAT	CARBS

LOW IN SATURATED FAT • LOW FAT

Serves: 6 (hearty lunch)   Prep Time: 15 mins   Cooking Time: 30 mins

---

HARIRA SOUP is a traditional Moroccan dish that's perfect for a warm and comforting meal – it's often served during Ramadan after the fast is broken. Our recipe is packed full of tangy spices, sweet apricots, and wholesome pulses.

CLIMATE KITCHEN HACKS we use chicken rather than beef or lamb and swap half of the chicken for butter beans. The same serving size has a 90% lower carbon footprint, 25% fewer calories, and 65% less saturated fat than beef-based recipes.

Super Soups

INGREDIENTS

- 8 sprays canola (rapeseed) oil
- 1 large onion (120g), finely chopped
- 3 cloves of garlic, minced/crushed
- 1 tbsp fresh ginger, finely sliced or grated
- 1 tsp ground cumin
- 1 tsp ground turmeric
- 1 tsp ground cinnamon
- 1 tsp paprika
- Salt and pepper, to taste
- 1/2 lb (1 cup, 250g) boneless chicken, cut into small pieces
- 1 can (400g, 220g dry weight) butter beans, drained
- 1 can (400g, 220g dry weight) chickpeas, drained
- 1/2 cup (120g) lentils, rinsed
- 6 medium sized tomatoes (2 cups, 480g), diced
- 4 cups (1L) chicken or vegetable broth/stock
- 1/4 cup (60g) sauce flour (or plain flour)
- 1-2 lemons (1/4 cup, 60ml) freshly squeezed
- 1/4 cup (40g) chopped fresh cilantro/coriander, to serve
- 2-4 tbsp apricots, roughly chopped, to serve

INSTRUCTIONS

1. Assemble, measure, and prepare the ingredients.
2. In a large pot, spray coat with 4 sprays of oil and heat over a medium heat. Add the onion and fry until softened (2-3 minutes), spray more oil and add the garlic and ginger for another 1 minute.
3. Turn the heat to low and add the cumin, turmeric, cinnamon, paprika, salt and pepper, spray more oil and sauté for another 1-2 minutes.
4. Add the chicken, butter beans, chickpeas, lentils, diced tomatoes, stir thoroughly, add the broth/stock, turn up the heat and bring to a boil. Reduce the heat to low, cover, and simmer for about 30 minutes or until the chicken is cooked through and the lentils and chickpeas are tender.
5. Meanwhile, in a small bowl mix the sauce flour with half a cup (120ml) of cold water and stir into a smooth paste.
6. Return to the soup and adjust the seasoning, then gradually add the flour/water mix whilst constantly stirring until you get the desired thickness (remember as it cools it will thicken a little extra you may not need all the flour mix). Let the flour cook out for 2-3 minutes (to avoid raw flour taste). Turn off the heat.
7. Stir in half the lemon juice, taste, add more if required.
8. Serve the Harira Soup hot, garnishing with cilantro/coriander and apricots.

CHICKEN CAESAR SALAD

EACH SERVING

330g	360	35%	40%	25%
CARBON	CALORIES	PROTEIN	FAT	CARBS

HIGH PROTEIN

Serves: 4 (light lunch)   Prep Time: 15 mins

CAESAR SALAD wasn't invented by Julius Caesar but rather Caesar Cardini, an Italian chef working in Mexico in the 1920s. Our recipe has a fresh, light, and tangy dressing to compliment the crispy leaves, rich chicken, and sumptuous eggs. Perfect as a side or a light lunch and fit for a king (or an emperor).

CLIMATE KITCHEN HACKS we switch half the mayo to reduced fat mayo and replace the other half with plain soy yogurt. We take some of the parmesan out of the dressing and sprinkle a little on top to deliver a punch of taste whilst using less hard cheese. The same serving size has a 30% lower carbon footprint, 35% fewer calories, and 60% less fat than regular chicken Caesar salad recipes.

INGREDIENTS

- 2 medium/large eggs, at room temperature
- 1 clove garlic, whole
- 1/2 cup (60ml) reduced fat mayonnaise
- 1/2 cup (60ml) plain soy yogurt (or natural yogurt if you prefer the taste)
- 1/4 cup (25g) grated Parmesan cheese
- 1/2 lemon, freshly squeezed
- 1 tsp Dijon mustard
- 1 tsp Worcestershire sauce
- Salt and pepper, to taste
- 1 large (or 2 smaller) romaine lettuce (300g), washed and chopped
- 1 cup (240g) cooked chicken breast
- 6-8 anchovy fillets (30g), chopped
- 1/2 cup (40g) croutons
- Salt and pepper, to taste

INSTRUCTIONS

1. Bring a small pan of water to a boil, prick the blunt end of the eggs to allow the air to escape (avoids cracking during cooking), boil the eggs for 7 minutes to set the white and leave the yolk sticky. Once done, remove from the pan and place in cold water to cool and stop cooking.

2. Meanwhile, heat the unpeeled garlic clove in a skillet on a medium-high heat for 5 minutes to deactivate the enzyme that causes the very intense garlic hit and aftertaste. Remove from the skillet and mince/crush.

3. As the garlic heats, assemble, measure, and prepare the other ingredients.

4. In a small bowl, mix the mayo, yogurt, half the parmesan, half the lemon juice, garlic, mustard, Worcestershire sauce, and a pinch of salt & pepper. Taste and add more seasoning or lemon if required.

5. In a large bowl, mix the lettuce, cooked chicken, anchovies, half the croutons, and the Caesar dressing. Toss to coat. Peel and quarter the boiled eggs.

6. Place the salad in serving bowl/s and place the quartered boiled eggs and remaining croutons on top, sprinkle with the remaining Parmesan cheese to finish.

MINTED GREEK SALAD

EACH SERVING

280g	180	15%	60%	25%
CARBON	CALORIES	PROTEIN	FAT	CARBS

LOW CALORIE • VEGETARIAN

Serves: 4 (light lunch)   Prep Time: 15 mins

GREEK SALAD is a fresh and delicious dish that's perfect as a side dish or a light lunch. With salty feta and olives, sweet tomatoes, and bitter lettuce this simple salad delivers big on taste. We add a sprinkling of mint to balance that salty, creamy feta.

CLIMATE KITCHEN HACKS Greek salad is a great low carbon dish with plenty of vegetables. The feta cheese does have a high fat and saturated fat content (though lower than many other cheeses). You may wish to opt for a reduced fat feta or eat in moderation. We go easy on the feta by crumbling half to disperse the taste and dicing the other half to give that intense salty-feta hit.

Sensational Salads

INGREDIENTS

- 1 clove of garlic, whole
- 1 large or 2 smaller romaine lettuce (300g), washed and chopped
- 1 large tomato (1 cup, 200g), diced
- 1/2 a large cucumber (1 1/2 cup, 150g), diced
- 1/2 red onion (1/2 cup, 120g), halved/or quartered and thin sliced
- 1/4 cup (60g) of Kalamata olives, pitted and halved
- 1/2 cup (120g) of feta cheese, 1/2 crumbled and 1/2 diced
- 1 tbsp olive oil
- 1 tbsp red wine vinegar
- Salt and pepper, to taste
- 2-4 tbsp fresh mint leaves, chopped, to serve

INSTRUCTIONS

1. Heat the unpeeled garlic clove in a skillet/pan on a medium-high heat for 5 minutes to deactivate the enzyme that causes the very intense garlic hit and aftertaste. Remove from the skillet/pan and mince/crush.
2. Whilst the garlic heats, assemble, measure, and prepare the ingredients.
3. In a large bowl, mix the lettuce, tomato, cucumber, red onion, olives, and feta cheese.
4. In a small bowl, whisk together the olive oil, red wine vinegar, and garlic. Add salt and pepper to taste.
5. Pour the dressing over the salad and toss to coat evenly. Sprinkle the mint over the top.

BEETROOT NIÇOISE SALAD

EACH SERVING

| 400g | 280 | 25% | 35% | 40% |
| CARBON | CALORIES | PROTEIN | FAT | CARBS |

Serves: 4 (light lunch) Prep Time: 10 mins Cooking Time: 40 mins

NIÇOISE SALAD is a classic French dish that's perfect for a light lunch or a summery side dish. We add roasted beetroot to create a delicious balance against the salty olives, savory tuna, and sweet tomatoes.

CLIMATE KITCHEN HACKS go easy on the eggs to avoid the added saturated fat. Instead, we add roasted fresh beetroot to create a sweet earthy undertone and a healthy source of protein. The same serving size has a 10% lower carbon footprint, 10% fewer calories, 25% less fat, and 40% less saturated fat than regular Niçoise recipes.

Sensational Salads

INGREDIENTS

- 1 cup (240g) of small/baby/new potatoes, halved (no need to peel)
- 1 cup (240g) fresh beetroot/beet, thickly sliced (slightly smaller than the potato halves)
- 4 sprays canola (rapeseed) oil
- 2 eggs
- 1/2 cup (120g) of green beans, trimmed and halved
- 2 tbsp of balsamic glaze (or vinegar for a thinner dressing)
- 1 tbsp olive oil
- Salt and pepper, to taste
- 1 head of butter lettuce, chopped
- 1/2 cup (100g) of cherry tomatoes, halved
- 1/2 cup (100g) of Niçoise olives, pitted
- 4 oz (115g) of canned skipjack tuna in water, drained (sustainably caught)

INSTRUCTIONS

1. Preheat a fan assisted oven to 400°F / 200°C / Gas mark 6 (for non-fan oven 425°F / 220°C / Gas mark 7).
2. Assemble, measure, and prepare the ingredients.
3. Place the halved potatoes and thickly sliced beetroot into a roasting tray, lightly spray with oil to coat and roast in the oven for about 25-30 mins (toss the beets and potatoes half-way through cooking and spray a little more oil if the veg looks too dry). Cook until the potatoes are crispy and the beets caramelized around the edges. Remove from the oven and leave to cool.
4. Bring a small pan of water to a boil, prick the blunt end of the eggs to allow the air to escape (avoids cracking during cooking), boil the eggs for 7 minutes to set the white and leave the yolk sticky. Once done, remove from the pan and place in cold water to cool and stop cooking. Reserve the hot water from the pan.
5. Use the boiling water from the egg pan to boil the green beans for 5 minutes until slightly softened but still retaining a little crunch. Leave the beans to cool in cold or iced water.
6. In a small bowl, whisk together the balsamic and olive oil. Taste and add salt and pepper as required.
7. Ensure the potatoes, beetroot, eggs, and beans have cooled. Peel and quarter the boiled eggs. Assemble the salad by combining the potatoes, beetroot, green beans, lettuce, tomatoes, olives and tuna.
8. Pour the dressing over the salad and toss to coat evenly. In a large bowl or individual bowls serve the salad with the quartered egg on top.

WALDORF SALAD

EACH SERVING

240g	400	5%	50%	45%
CARBON	CALORIES	PROTEIN	FAT	CARBS

VEGETARIAN • VEGAN OPTION

Serves: 4 (light lunch)   Prep Time: 15 mins   Cooking Time: 30 mins

WALDORF SALAD is a classic dish whose origins date back over a century, created by the maître d' at the Waldorf-Astoria hotel in New York. It's the perfect salad for a light lunch, or as a wholesome side, with a great balance of rich nuts and sweet versus bitter flavors. A delightful tastebud brawl between honey vs vinegar, grapes vs lemons and sultanas vs watercress.

CLIMATE KITCHEN HACKS we use reduced fat mayonnaise to save on the calories and saturated fat. We also switch the sour cream for soy or oat yogurt to lower the carbon footprint. The same serving size has a 30% lower carbon footprint, 30% fewer calories, 50% less fat, and 60% less saturated fat than regular Waldorf salad recipes.

INGREDIENTS

- 2 cups (400g) small red apples, finely sliced or diced (skin on)
- 1 cup (240g) celery, finely sliced or diced
- 1 cup (200ml) grapes, halved
- 1 cup (100g) walnuts, roughly chopped
- 1/4 cup (60g) reduced fat mayonnaise (or vegan option)
- 1/2 cup (120g) oat-based crème fraiche or yogurt (or soy if you prefer)
- 1 tbsp honey
- 1 tsp fresh lemon juice (1/2 a small lemon)
- Salt and pepper, to taste
- 2 tbsp water cress, to serve
- 2 tbsp sultanas, to serve

INSTRUCTIONS

1. Assemble, measure, and prepare the ingredients. After you slice the apple squeeze a little lemon juice over to prevent browning of the flesh.
2. In a large bowl, combine the diced apples, celery, grapes, and chopped walnuts. Reserve a handful to serve.
3. In a small bowl, mix the mayonnaise, oat/soy crème fraiche, honey, and half the lemon juice. Season with salt and pepper to taste and add more lemon juice if required.
4. Pour the dressing over the apple mixture and stir until well combined.
5. Plate up and sprinkle the reserved salad mix on top (the undressed ingredients look more appealing).
6. Refrigerate for at least 30 minutes before serving to allow the flavors to meld together.
7. Serve chilled with water cress and sultanas sprinkled over the top.

AVOCADO CAPRESE SALAD

EACH SERVING

400g	270	15%	70%	15%
CARBON	CALORIES	PROTEIN	FAT	CARBS

VEGETARIAN

Serves: 4 (light lunch)   Prep Time: 15 mins

CAPRESE SALAD is a classic Italian dish that's simple, fresh and perfect for summertime!

CLIMATE KITCHEN HACKS switch half the mozzarella for avocado and reduce the olive oil content to save on carbon emissions and fat. The same serving size has a 30% lower carbon footprint, 30% fewer calories, and 30% less fat than regular salad Caprese.

Sensational Salads

INGREDIENTS

- 4 large tomatoes (1lb, 450g), sliced
- 1/4 cup of fresh basil, leaves separated
- 1 ball of fresh mozzarella cheese (120g), sliced
- 1 large avocado (1 cup, 180g), sliced
- 2 tbsp of extra virgin olive oil
- 1 tbsp of balsamic vinegar
- Salt and pepper, to taste

INSTRUCTIONS

1. Assemble, measure, and prepare the ingredients.
2. In a large platter, layer the ingredients: tomato slice, basil leaf, mozzarella slice, avocado slice, tomato slice, basil leaf, mozzarella slice, avocado slice and so on....
3. Next in a small bowl, mix the olive oil and balsamic vinegar, season with salt and pepper to taste.
4. Drizzle the dressing over the salad.

SPICY THAI TUNA SALAD

EACH SERVING

400g	180	50%	25%	25%
CARBON	CALORIES	PROTEIN	FAT	CARBS

HIGH PROTEIN • LOW CALORIE

Serves: 4 (light lunch)   Prep Time: 15 mins   Cooking Time: 15 mins

---

THAI TUNA SALAD is perfect for those who crave a bit of spice. Sure to be a hit with everyone who loves Thai cuisine, this salad has a great balance of sweet and sour sauce with a spicy kick, topped off with the delicate sesame tuna served on top.

CLIMATE KITCHEN HACKS trying to choose low carbon fish options can leave you in murky waters. This dish is traditionally made with salmon which can have a carbon footprint as low as chicken or nearly as high as beef. Switching the salmon to a smaller portion of tuna is a more reliable sustainable choice. Oh, and we think it tastes even better. The same serving size has a 60% lower carbon footprint and 30% less fat than Thai salmon salad recipes.

Sensational Salads

INGREDIENTS

- 1/2 lb (225g) fresh yellowfin tuna steak/s (make sure MSC certified & sustainably sourced)
- 1 tbsp canola (rapeseed) oil
- 3-4 tbsp of sesame seeds (ideally black and white mixed)
- 4 cups (250g) of mixed green leaves (rocket or baby leaves taste great)
- 1 cup (240g) of cherry tomatoes, quartered
- 1/2 cucumber (1/2 cup, 120g), sliced
- 1/4 cup of cilantro/coriander, chopped
- 1/4 cup of mint, chopped
- 2 small limes (3 tbsp, 45ml), freshly squeezed
- 3 tbsp (45ml) of fish sauce
- 1 1/2 tbsp of brown sugar
- 1/2 - 2 tsp of siracha hot chili sauce
- Salt and pepper, to taste

INSTRUCTIONS

1. Assemble, measure, and prepare the ingredients. Be careful not to overpower the dish with heat from the hot chili sauce - generally 1/2 tsp will be warm, 1 tsp will have a kick, 2 tsp will be hot - you can always add more at the end.
2. First, take the raw tuna steak, cut each steak into 2 oblongs, and pat down with soft kitchen paper to remove the excess water. Spray with a little canola (rapeseed) oil on all sides. Spread the sesame seeds on a plate and dip the tuna steak into the seeds to coat all sides.
3. Heat 1 tbsp canola (rapeseed) oil in the middle of a non-stick skillet or heavy frying pan until smoking hot. Place the tuna steak onto the oil, tilt the pan to swill the oil against the tuna and/or gently press down with the back of a spatula until it starts to sizzle (be careful as hot sesame seeds will spit). Cook the tuna steak for exactly 30 seconds on each of the 4 long sides of the oblong shape, then using some tongs quickly hold the steaks upright to sear the 2 smaller ends on the hot pan. Take care to watch the clock as these timings should yield the perfect medium-rare tuna with seared fish and toasted sesame seeds on the outside and pink flesh in the middle (cook for an extra 1 minute if you don't like rare tuna). Once the time is up, remove the tuna steak from the pan to stop the cooking. Set aside to cool.
4. In a large bowl, combine the mixed greens, cherry tomatoes, cucumber, cilantro/coriander, and mint.
5. In a small bowl, mix the lime juice, fish sauce, brown sugar, and siracha hot chili sauce. Season with salt and pepper to taste.
6. Reserve a handful of the salad mix, then drizzle half the dressing over the remainder of the salad and toss well to coat. Taste and add more dressing, salt & pepper, or hot chili sauce as required.
7. Cut the tuna into slices using a very sharp knife (to prevent flaking apart).
8. Serve the salad in bowls with the reserved salad leaves and sesame tuna slices scattered on top (the salad leaves without dressing look more appealing).

SWEET PAPAYA THAI SALAD

EACH SERVING

280g	250	15%	35%	50%
CARBON	CALORIES	PROTEIN	FAT	CARBS

LOW CALORIE • LOW IN SATURATED FAT • BALANCED MACRONUTRIENTS • VEGETARIAN

Serves: 4 (light lunch)   Prep Time: 15 mins   Cooking Time: 10 mins

---

THAI PAPAYA SALAD also known as "Som Tum," is a delicious and refreshing dish that's perfect for hot summer days. However, the green (unripe) papaya used in traditional Som Tum contains an enzyme called papain which can create adverse side-effects when eaten. In our version of this recipe we use ripened papaya which is softer, easier to buy, and does not contain the harmful enzyme. Our version of the salad is packed with Thai umami seasoning, sweet papaya, and delicious crunchy fresh veggies.

CLIMATE KITCHEN HACKS no hacks needed for this blockbuster. Our sweet papaya Thai salad is bursting with flavor, provides a great balance of macronutrients, and all with a small carbon footprint.

INGREDIENTS

- 2 cups (480g) of ripe but firm papaya (or mango), peeled, deseeded and julienned or shredded
- 2 large carrots (1 cup, 200g), peeled and julienned or shredded
- 1/2 cup (200g) of mange tout/sugar pea, julienned or shredded
- 1/4 cup of cilantro/coriander, chopped
- 1/2 cup (120g) of cherry tomatoes, quartered
- 2 tbsp of lime juice
- 2 tbsp of fish sauce
- 1 tbsp of brown sugar
- 1-2 tsp siracha, hot chili sauce
- 1/4 cup (70g) of dry roasted peanuts, roughly chopped
- Salt and pepper, to taste
- Mandoline slicer (optional but helpful)

INSTRUCTIONS

1. Assemble, measure, and prepare the ingredients. You can julienne (cut into matchstick thick strips) or shred the vegetables using a knife, however a mandoline slicer is faster if you have one. Be careful not to overpower the dish with heat from the hot chili sauce, generally 1/2 tsp will be warm, 1 tsp will have a kick, 2 tsp will be hot - you can always add more at the end.
2. In a large bowl, combine the carrots, mange tout/sugar pea, and cilantro/coriander. Lightly crush the ingredients with a pestle (or the end of a rolling pin or back of a fork) to release the flavors. Add the cherry tomatoes and papaya.
3. In a small bowl, mix the lime juice, fish sauce, brown sugar, and hot chili sauce. Drizzle the dressing over the salad mixture and toss well to coat. Add the chopped peanuts and toss again.
4. Season with salt and pepper and more hot sauce (if you need it) to taste.
5. Place in the refrigerator and let the flavors infuse. Serve Chilled.

NOT-FRIED CHICKEN BURGERS

EACH SERVING

| 540g | 600 | 29% | 31% | 40% |
| CARBON | CALORIES | PROTEIN | FAT | CARBS |

Serves: 4   Prep Time: 15 mins   Cooking Time: 15 mins

FRIED CHICKEN who doesn't love it? But what we don't love is the oil, calories, and saturated fat. Well try these Not-Fried Chicken Burgers; they are fluffy, crunchy and juicy - and we think better than your favorite chicken-shop fried chicken.

CLIMATE KITCHEN HACKS our not-fried chicken burgers are cooked in the oven rather than shallow or deep fried. For amazingly crispy, succulent chicken the trick is to use fluffy panko breadcrumbs, to cook on a wire rack in a hot oven, and to use just a light spray of oil to ensure an even cook and stop the breadcrumbs burning. The same serving size has a 20% lower carbon footprint, 35% fewer calories, and up to 55% less fat than shallow fried crispy chicken burgers.

INGREDIENTS

- 1/4 cup (30g) all-purpose flour
- 1 tsp paprika
- 1 tsp garlic granules
- Salt and pepper, to taste
- 1 egg, beaten
- 1 cup (50g) panko breadcrumbs
- 1 lb (450g) raw chicken tenders/mini-fillets/goujons (smaller than chicken breasts)
- 8 sprays canola (rapeseed) oil
- 4 burger buns
- Lettuce, tomato, and your favorite burger toppings.
- A wire rack for cooking

INSTRUCTIONS

1. Preheat the fan oven to 430°F / 220°C / Gas mark 7 with a large baking tray inside (for non-fan oven 465°F / 240°C / Gas mark 8).
2. Assemble, measure, and prepare the ingredients.
3. In a shallow dish, mix the flour, paprika, garlic granules, and a pinch of salt & pepper. In another shallow dish, beat the egg. In a third shallow dish, place the panko breadcrumbs.
4. Dip each chicken tender into the flour mixture, then the beaten egg, and finally coat it with panko breadcrumbs. Spray both sides of the chicken tenders with canola (rapeseed) oil to lightly coat. Arrange on a wire rack.
5. Remove the hot baking tray from the oven and place the wire rack with the chicken tenders on the tray. Place in the oven and cook for 15-20 minutes, turning halfway through. Test the least cooked piece of chicken to check if cooked (it should be white in the center when cut in half).
6. As the chicken cooks, toast the inside of the burger buns on a griddle pan or grill, assemble the burgers with chicken tenders, lettuce, tomato, and your favorite toppings.

HAM-BURGER & FRIES

EACH SERVING

560g	730	25%	20%	55%
CARBON	CALORIES	PROTEIN	FAT	CARBS

Serves: 4   Prep Time: 15 mins   Cooking Time: 30 mins

HAMBURGERS weirdly, aren't made from ham - they are made from beef (the name comes from where the dish originated in Hamburg, Germany). Well, this recipe is a real Ham-Burger made with pork, and we think it tastes even better than the original!

CLIMATE KITCHEN HACKS we switch the beef for pork, add some grated beetroot and a sprinkle of paprika to get the same great taste of a beef burger without the carbon emissions. The beetroot keeps the burger beautifully moist, gives a deliciously earthy flavor to the pork, and creates that medium-rare beefburger look. The same serving size has a whopper (excuse the pun) 90% lower carbon footprint, 20% fewer calories, and 40% less fat than a regular beef-based hamburger.

Comfort Foods

INGREDIENTS

- 4 potatoes (600g), scrubbed and cut into fries
- 1 lb (450g) ground/minced pork
- 1/2 cup (100g) fresh beetroot, grated
- 1 tbsp breadcrumbs
- 2 tsp paprika
- Salt and pepper
- 8 sprays canola (rapeseed) oil
- 4 burger buns
- 1 red onion (1 cup, 200g), halved and sliced
- A pinch of sugar
- Lettuce, tomato, and your favorite burger sauces.

INSTRUCTIONS

1. Preheat the fan oven to 425ºF / 220ºC / Gas mark 7 (for a non-fan oven 465ºF / 240ºC / Gas mark 8).
2. First, cut the potatoes into fries and place in a bowl of cold salty water to draw the moisture from the potato and help the fries crisp up.
3. Assemble, measure, and prepare the other ingredients.
4. In a large bowl, mix the ground pork, beetroot, breadcrumbs, and 1 tsp paprika with a pinch of salt and pepper. Using your hands, shape the mix into four thick patties about the size of your palm.
5. Drain the fries and pat dry with a tea-towel or soft kitchen paper. Spread the dry fries evenly over a large baking tray (make sure they have plenty of space on the tray to ensure they go crispy), spray with 4 sprays of the oil to coat, sprinkle over 1 tsp paprika, salt and pepper. Place in the pre-heated oven for 25 minutes until cooked through and crisp.
6. Immediately after putting the fries in the oven, heat a griddle pan (or frying pan) to high heat. Griddle/fry the burgers for 2-3 minutes per side to seal the outside and create griddle marks. Transfer the burgers to the oven with the fries for 20 minutes to cook through (don't worry they won't dry out like beefburgers thanks to the beetroot). The burgers are done when the meat is springy to the touch (it returns to shape) - the juices will run a pink color like a rare beef burger due to the beetroot coloring.
7. As the burgers and fries cook in the oven, heat a pan on a low heat with a spray of oil and add the sliced red onion and a pinch of sugar to slowly fry and caramelize the onion whilst the fries/burgers cook (15 mins or so).
8. Toast the burger buns on the griddle pan. Once ready, assemble the burgers and stack with caramelized onion, lettuce, tomato, and your favorite sauces.
9. Serve the burgers with the fries on the side.

THREE CHEESE MAC & CHEESE

EACH SERVING

730g	790	18%	34%	48%
CARBON	CALORIES	PROTEIN	FAT	CARBS

VEGETARIAN

Serves: 4   Prep Time: 10 mins   Cooking Time: 30 mins

MAC & CHEESE is so much better when cooked and eaten fresh. Restaurants often refrigerate and reheat mac & cheese but this causes the pasta to absorb all the moisture and flavor of the cheese sauce making the dish dry and bland. Our fresh version uses nutty gruyere cheese sauce and is topped with a delightfully crispy crumb - we guarantee you will be coming back for more.

CLIMATE KITCHEN HACKS Mac & Cheese is one of the best comfort foods out there, but it does contain lots of dairy. Our recipe switches a portion of the semi-soft cheese for a smaller amount of very strong flavored hard cheese like parmesan and gruyere. This maintains the creamy texture, adds extra flavor, but reduces the carbon footprint, calories, and fat. The same serving size has a 25% lower carbon footprint, 5% fewer calories, and 30% less fat than a regular mac and cheese.

Comfort Foods

INGREDIENTS

- 12 oz (350g) elbow macaroni
- 2 tbsp (30g) butter
- 3 tbsp sauce flour (or all-purpose flour)
- 2 cups (480ml) semi-skimmed milk
- 1 1/2 cup (180g) grated/shredded cheddar cheese
- 1 tsp mustard powder
- 1/2 cup (30g) gruyere cheese, grated/shredded
- Salt and pepper, to taste
- 3 tbsp (20g) parmesan, finely grated/shredded
- 3 tbsp (20g) breadcrumbs
- 6 sprays olive oil
- A handful of chopped cherry tomatoes/spring/green onions/basil leaves, to serve (optional)

INSTRUCTIONS

1. Assemble, measure, and prepare the ingredients.
2. Cook the macaroni according to package instructions leaving a little bite to it (al dente). Drain and set aside.
3. Meanwhile, in a large pan, melt the butter over a low heat (don't be tempted to turn the heat up as this will burn the flour). Add the flour 1 tbsp at a time and stir with a wooden spoon until all incorporated. Continue stirring for 1-2 minutes or until the mixture turns slightly golden.
4. Next, slowly pour the milk into the flour mix, first 1 tbsp at a time, then you can gradually add bigger and bigger portions - stir constantly. Keep the heat low or the mix will split and flour burn (if the mix splits into lumps you can sprinkle over a little more flour and stir like crazy to recover the smooth paste). The mix will turn very thick like mashed potato as you first add the milk and then end up like a thin custard consistency.
5. Once all the milk has been added, stir in the cheddar cheese, mustard powder, gruyere cheese, salt, and pepper. Cook on low until the cheese is melted and the sauce is smooth.
6. Preheat the broiler/grill to medium hot.
7. Place the breadcrumbs in a bowl and spray over 6 sprays of olive oil, mixing between each spray to make a crumb.
8. Once the cheese sauce is ready, add to the cooked macaroni pasta and toss to coat. Transfer to a heat proof dish, sprinkle over the breadcrumb crumb and grated parmesan and place under the grill/broiler until the breadcrumbs turn golden.
9. Serve hot with a sprinkle of chopped green/spring onion, cherry tomato, or basil on top.

PIRI PIRI CHICKEN & CORN CUTLETS

EACH SERVING

450g	790	30%	35%	35%
CARBON	CALORIES	PROTEIN	FAT	CARBS

HIGH IN PROTEIN

- Serves: 4
- Marinate Time: 120 mins
- Prep Time: 10 mins
- Cooking Time: 30 mins

PIRI PIRI is an African bird's eye chili which measures about an inch long but packs a big punch. The chilies are used to create this weeknight classic of spicy chicken, juicy corn riblets, and moreish potato wedges. The ultimate comfort food night in.

CLIMATE KITCHEN HACKS Piri Piri Chicken is best made with flavorful cuts of meat such as chicken thighs or drumsticks which have a lower carbon footprint than chicken breast. Spray rather than drizzle the oil and the same serving size has a 50% lower carbon footprint, 10% fewer calories, and 30% less fat than regular recipes with chicken breast and excess oil.

Comfort Foods

INGREDIENTS

- 2 tbsp olive oil
- 4 tbsp red wine vinegar
- 3 cloves of garlic, minced/crushed
- 2-4 bird's eye chili peppers (ideally piri piri but any birds eye will work), seeded and finely chopped
- 2 tsp smoked paprika
- 1 tsp cumin
- 1 tsp oregano
- Salt and pepper
- 8 large chicken thighs or drumsticks (800g),
- 4 corn on the cob
- 4 potatoes (600g), peeled and cut into 8-12 wedges each
- 1 tsp paprika
- 8 sprays canola (rapeseed) oil
- Salt and pepper, to taste
- 4 tbsp cilantro/coriander, chopped, to serve

INSTRUCTIONS

1. Assemble, measure, and prepare the ingredients. Use two bird's eye chilies for warmth, three for a kick, and four or more if you like your piri piri hot!
2. In a large bowl, mix the olive oil, red wine vinegar, garlic, red chili peppers, smoked paprika, cumin, oregano, and a pinch of salt and pepper.
3. Add the chicken and corn to the sauce and toss to coat. Cover and refrigerate for at least 2 hours or overnight to marinade.
4. Preheat a fan oven to 410ºF / 210ºC / Gas mark 7 (for a non-fan oven 450ºF / 230ºC / Gas mark 8).
5. Carefully chop the corn on the cob in half lengthways and then chop each half into quarters lengthways. This requires a very sharp knife and steady hands - only do it if you are confident - you can leave the cobs whole if preferred.
6. Spread the potato wedges over a large baking tray, sprinkle over the paprika, and spray coat with oil. Place in the oven for 25-30 minutes until crispy, turn halfway through cooking using a spatula to loosen the wedges from the tray.
7. As soon as the wedges are in the oven, place the marinated chicken and corn riblets on a baking tray, spray coat with oil, and cook in the same oven for about 20-25 minutes.
8. Serve the piri piri chicken hot with wedges and corn riblets. Garnish with cilantro/coriander.
9. If you want dipping sauce to accompany the dish, try mixing Siracha hot sauce with vegan mayo for some added zing.

SMOKY CHICKEN FAJITAS

EACH SERVING

760g	760	20%	40%	40%
CARBON	CALORIES	PROTEIN	FAT	CARBS

Serves: 4 Prep Time: 10 mins Cooking Time: 15 mins

FAJITAS are often thought to be a Mexican classic, but they actually started out in the US in the 1970s. Mexican restaurants in Texas started marinating spare cuts of beef and serving it up in a tortilla roll. Our version of fajitas combines juicy chicken, smoky bell pepper and onion slices, all wrapped up in a deliciously fluffy tortilla.

CLIMATE KITCHEN HACKS we switch some chicken for avocado and use natural yogurt rather than sour cream to reduce the carbon footprint of the dish. The same serving size has a 10% lower carbon footprint than regular chicken fajitas and a 90% smaller carbon footprint when compared to steak fajitas.

INGREDIENTS

Tomato Salsa:
- 1 cup (240g) tomatoes, diced
- 1/4 cup (60g) green/spring onion, finely sliced
- 1 tbsp olive oil
- 1 tsp white wine vinegar

Fajitas:
- 2 tbsp canola (rapeseed) oil
- 2 cloves of garlic, minced
- 1-3 tsp mild chili powder
- 1 tsp cumin
- 1 tsp smoked paprika
- Salt and pepper, to taste
- 1 lb (400g) raw chicken breast, sliced
- 1 red pepper (1 cup/240g), sliced
- 1 yellow/or green pepper (1 cup/240g), sliced
- 1 large onion (1 cup/240g), sliced
- 8-12 flour or corn tortillas
- 4 tbsp (60ml) plain natural yogurt
- 1 avocado (140g), peeled and sliced
- Lime wedges, to serve
- Coriander/cilantro, chopped, to serve

INSTRUCTIONS

1. Assemble, measure, and prepare the ingredients.
2. In a small bowl combine the tomatoes, green/spring onions, olive oil and vinegar for the tomato salsa. Mix and set aside to marinade.
3. In a large bowl, mix the oil, garlic, chili powder, cumin, smoked paprika, and a pinch of salt and pepper. Add the chicken and toss to coat.
4. Heat a large skillet or griddle over high heat. Add a spray of oil and the chicken and cook for about 7-8 minutes until browned and cooked through (test the thickest piece of chicken and make sure it is white through to the middle).
5. Remove the chicken from the pan and set aside.
6. In the same pan, add the peppers and onions, spray with oil, and cook for about 3-4 minutes or until softened.
7. Warm the tortillas in the oven, microwave, or skillet.
8. Assemble the fajitas by placing the chicken, peppers, onions, and avocado on the tortillas. Add a spoonful of tomato salsa, natural yogurt, and a sprinkling of coriander/cilantro.
9. Roll up the tortillas, serve extra salsa and a lime wedge on the side.

SPICY BEAN BURRITOS

EACH SERVING

350g	520	13%	16%	71%
CARBON	CALORIES	PROTEIN	FAT	CARBS

VEGAN • LOW FAT

Serves: 4   Prep Time: 10 mins   Cooking Time: 15 mins

BURRITO means "little donkey" in Spanish. Nobody quite knows why this Mexican classic took the name burrito, though some think it derives from the fact that the tortilla carries lots of filling, just as the donkey carries heavy loads. What we do know is these vegan friendly bean burritos have a delicious and healthy combination of fleshy jackfruit, spicy beans, and crispy lettuce served with a sumptuous cashew melt.

CLIMATE KITCHEN HACKS we replace the cheese with delicious sweet potato and cashew melt. We use jackfruit with the beans to give added texture, bite, and flavor retention. The same serving size has a 70% lower carbon footprint, 40% fewer calories, and 70% less fat and saturated fat compared to regular bean burritos with cheese.

Comfort Foods

INGREDIENTS

- 2 sweet potatoes (240g), whole
- 1 can (15 oz/ 400g (200g drained)) young green jackfruit, drained and rinsed
- 1 can (15 oz/ 400g (200g drained)) black beans, drained and rinsed
- 2 cloves of garlic, minced/crushed
- 1-3 tsp mild chili powder
- 2 tsp cumin
- 2 cup (480 ml) vegetable broth/stock
- Salt and pepper, to taste
- 1/4 cup (60g) cashews (fairtrade certified)
- 4 large flour or corn tortillas
- 1 cup (240g) shredded iceberg lettuce
- 1 cup (240g) cooked rice

INSTRUCTIONS

1. Assemble, measure, and prepare the ingredients. Use 1 tsp of mild chili powder for warmth, 2 tsp for a kick, and 3 or more for hot burritos.
2. Prick the sweet potato (skin on) with a fork and microwave for 5-7 minutes (800W power) until soft.
3. Take the drained jackfruit and place inside soft kitchen paper or an old tea-towel and gently bash with a rolling pin - this will break-up the tougher parts of the jack fruit and partly dry the fruit so it can absorb all the flavors from the dish.
4. In a medium saucepan, heat the beans, jackfruit, garlic, chili powder, cumin, 1 cup of the vegetable broth/stock, and a pinch of salt and pepper over a medium heat (uncovered) for about 10 minutes, stirring occasionally, until the sauce has thickened.
5. Meanwhile, scoop out the cooked sweet potato insides and mix with the cashews and a 1/2 cup of the vegetable broth/stock in a blender (a hand blender works best), pulse until smooth, adding the remaining 1/2 cup of vegetable stock as needed to make a smooth, thick sauce.
6. Warm the tortillas in the oven, microwave, or in a skillet.
7. Assemble the burritos by placing 3 tbsp of bean mix, 3 tbsp of sweet potato melt, 2 tbsp of cooked rice, and a handful of shredded lettuce across the middle of a large tortilla. Fold the tortilla edge over the filling and tuck the edges in before rolling into a sealed cylinder. Repeat for each tortilla and cut in half to serve.

LIGHT & CRISPY TONKATSU PORK

EACH SERVING

700g	790	24%	21%	55%
CARBON	CALORIES	PROTEIN	FAT	CARBS

Serves: 4   Prep Time: 10 mins   Cooking Time: 25 mins

TONKATSU originated in Japan in the 19th century, a breaded, deep fried pork cutlet which is usually prepared for special occasions. Our recipe is super easy and delicious with crispy pork and a tangy sauce all served up with a sharp slaw to cut though the rich meat.

CLIMATE KITCHEN HACKS we use a lighter panko coating and oven cook rather than deep frying. The same serving size has a 20% lower carbon footprint, 15% fewer calories, and 40% less fat than deep fried recipes.

Comfort Foods

INGREDIENTS

- 4 boneless pork loin cutlets/steaks (500g)
- Salt and pepper, to taste
- 1/4 cup (30g) of all-purpose flour
- 1 egg, beaten
- 1 cup (75g) of panko breadcrumbs
- 8 sprays of canola (rapeseed) oil
- 1 1/2 cups (250g) rice, dry

For the slaw:

- 1/4 small green/savoy cabbage (1 cup, 150g), finely sliced or shredded
- 1 carrot (1/2 cup, 100g), julienned or shredded
- 1/2 lemon, freshly juiced
- 1 tsp caster sugar
- Salt and pepper, to taste

For the tonkatsu sauce:

- 1/2 cup (120ml) of tomato ketchup
- 2 tbsp (30ml) of Worcestershire sauce
- 2 tbsp (30ml) of oyster sauce
- 2 tbsp (30ml) of soy sauce
- 1 tbsp of sugar
- 1 tsp of Dijon mustard
- 1/4 cup (60ml) of water
- A wire rack for cooking

INSTRUCTIONS

1. Preheat a fan oven to 400°F / 200°C / Gas mark 6 with a large baking tray inside (for a non-fan oven 425°F / 220°C / Gas mark 7).
2. Assemble, measure, and prepare the ingredients. Season the pork cutlets with a pinch of salt and pepper.
3. Place the flour, egg, and panko breadcrumbs in three separate shallow bowls. Dredge the cutlets in the flour, then the egg, and finally coat with the panko breadcrumbs and spray each side with one spray of oil. Place the cutlets onto a wire rack and place the wire rack onto the hot baking tray in the oven. Cook for 20-25 minutes until golden brown and cooked through.
4. Meanwhile, cook the rice according to package instructions.
5. Whilst the rice and pork cook, prepare the slaw by mixing the shredded green cabbage, shredded carrots, lemon juice, and caster sugar into a large bowl and mixing well. Season with salt and pepper to taste, cover and leave the vegetables to soften in the acidic lemon juice.
6. Next, prepare the tonkatsu sauce. Mix the ketchup, Worcestershire sauce, oyster sauce, soy sauce, sugar, Dijon mustard, and water in a small saucepan and bring to a boil over a medium heat. Reduce the heat to low and simmer for 5-7 minutes until the sauce thickens.
7. Serve the tonkatsu pork cutlets over the rice with tonkatsu sauce on top and slaw on the side.

PORK BOLOGNESE

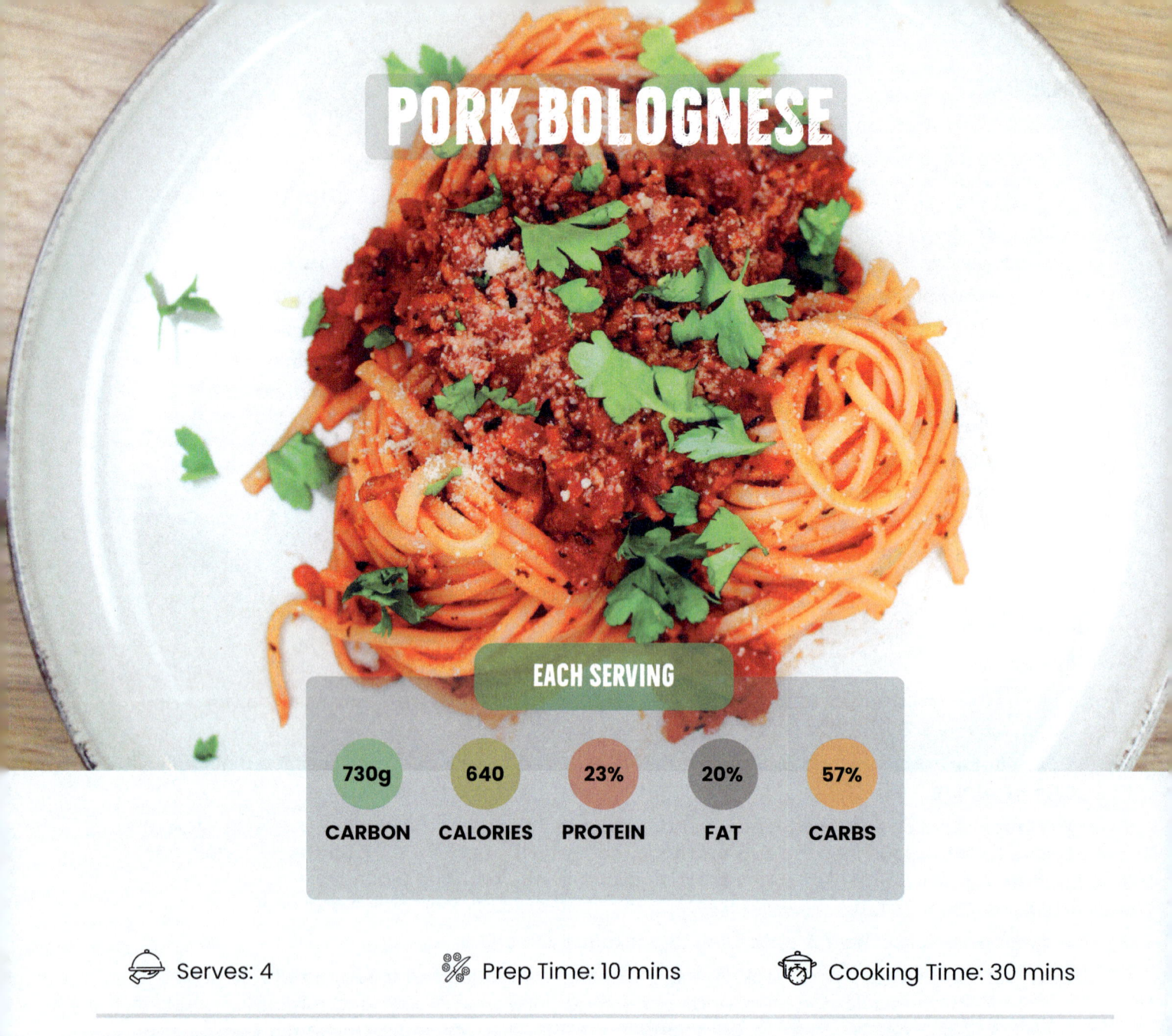

EACH SERVING

730g	640	23%	20%	57%
CARBON	CALORIES	PROTEIN	FAT	CARBS

Serves: 4   Prep Time: 10 mins   Cooking Time: 30 mins

SPAGHETTI BOLOGNESE is called ragu in Italy, and it is traditionally served on tagliatelle pasta, not spaghetti. Traditional Italian recipes use a mix of beef and pork pancetta. We go full pork in our version and add grated beetroot, to create a vibrant, rich, and tasty dish. Just don't spill it on your white shirt.

CLIMATE KITCHEN HACKS switch beef mince for pork mince and use pancetta and grated beet(root) to add color and depth of taste. Spray don't drizzle the oil. The same serving size has a 70% lower carbon footprint and 15% less fat than beef-based Bolognese recipes.

Perfect Pastas

INGREDIENTS

- 3/4 lb (340g) dry pasta (spaghetti, linguine)
- 1/2 cup (120g) of diced pancetta or pork lardons
- 1 medium onion (150g), finely diced
- 2 cloves of garlic, minced
- 1/2 lb (225g) of ground/minced pork
- 1 medium beet(root) (1/2 cup, 100g), grated (no need to peel)
- 2 tins (28 oz/800g) of crushed tomatoes (ideally 1 plum and 1 regular tin)
- 1/2 cup (120ml) of red wine
- 1 tbsp Worcestershire sauce
- 1 tbsp balsamic vinegar
- 2 tsp of dried basil
- 1 tsp of dried oregano
- Salt and pepper, to taste
- 2 tbsp Parmesan cheese, grated to serve
- 2 tbsp parsley/or basil, chopped, to serve

INSTRUCTIONS

1. Assemble, measure, and prepare the ingredients.
2. Cook the spaghetti according to package instructions, drain, and reserve. Coat the cooked pasta with one spray of olive oil to stop it sticking together.
3. Whilst the spaghetti cooks, take a large heavy pan and heat on medium-high. Add the pancetta/lardons and cook until starting to crisp and turn brown (2-3 mins, no need for extra oil as the pork will release its own fat). Next add the onion and cook until the onion is starting to soften (2-3 mins), add the garlic and fry for another 30 seconds.
4. Add the ground pork mince and grated beet(root) and cook until the mince is lightly browned (4-6 mins). Stir in the canned tomatoes, red wine, Worcestershire sauce, balsamic vinegar, dry basil, and oregano. Bring the mixture to a simmer.
5. Let the sauce simmer (uncovered) for at least 20 minutes, or until thickened and turned a deep red/brown color. Season with salt and pepper to taste.
6. Mix half the sauce with the spaghetti, serve the pasta by using a large fork and tablespoon to twirl the pasta into domes. Spoon the remainder of the sauce over the top. Garnish with Parmesan cheese and fresh parsley or basil.

CLASSIC PASTA CARBONARA

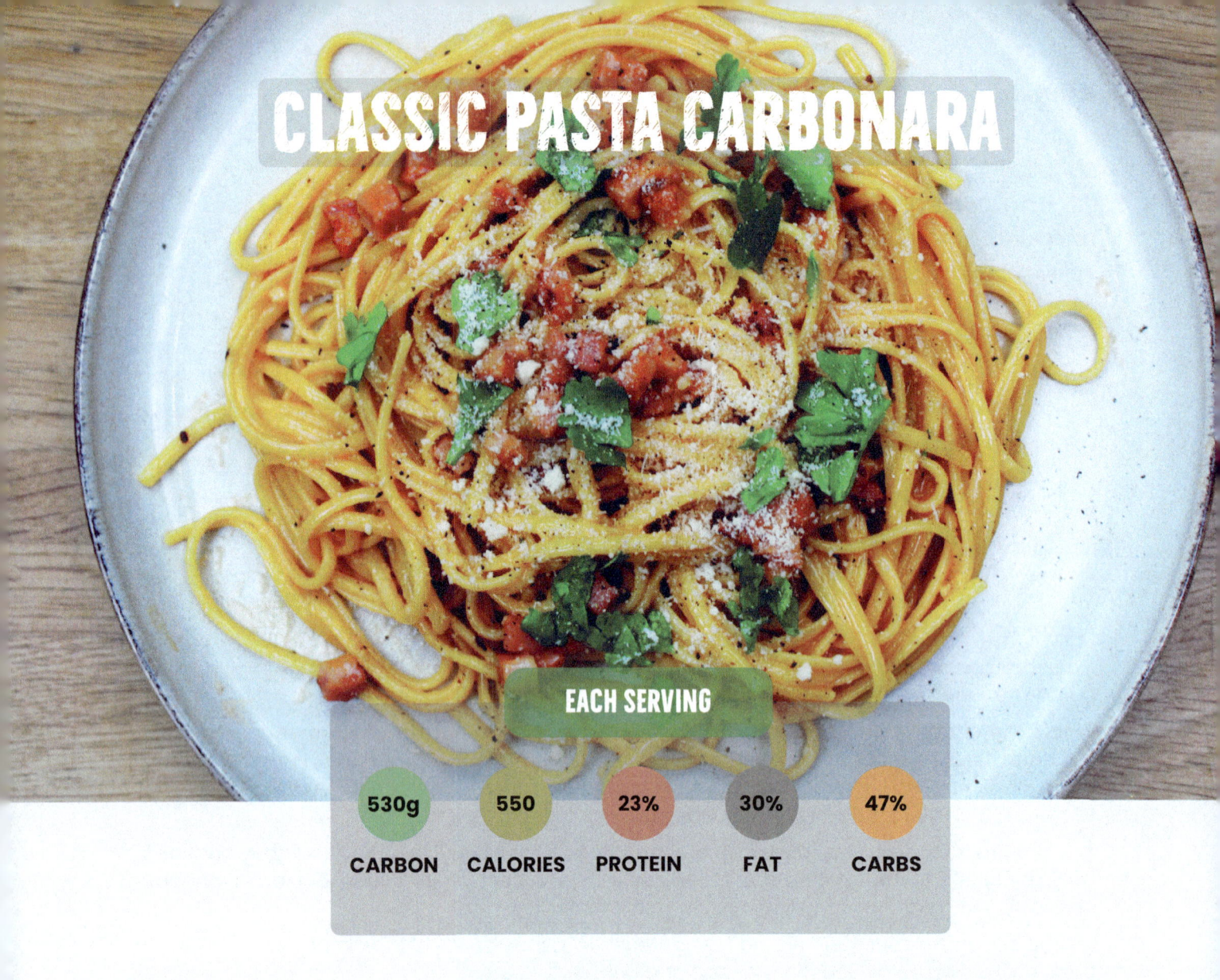

EACH SERVING

530g	550	23%	30%	47%
CARBON	CALORIES	PROTEIN	FAT	CARBS

Serves: 4   Prep Time: 10 mins   Cooking Time: 20 mins

CARBONARA according to some, was invented in northern Italy by a secret sect called the "Carboneria". Others believe it was devised by Italian restaurants to help stationed US-British troops to turn their egg and bacon rations into a delicious meal. Whatever the truth, carbonara is a now a classic recipe with creamy pasta, smoky pancetta, and rich Parmesan cheese. Quick, easy, and delicious any night of the week.

CLIMATE KITCHEN HACKS carbonara is a classic Italian dish that already has a low carbon footprint thanks to the use of pork pancetta as a flavor enhancer rather than bulk ingredient. A delicious dish that is easy to prepare. Avoid the unnecessary cooking oil and this carbonara has 20% less fat than traditional recipes.

INGREDIENTS

- 3/4 lb (340g) dry pasta (spaghetti or linguine)
- 1/2 cup (120g) of diced pancetta or pork lardons
- 4 cloves of garlic, minced
- 4 medium eggs
- 1 cup (100g) of grated Parmesan cheese
- Salt and pepper, to taste
- 2 tbsp grated Parmesan cheese, to serve
- 2 tbsp parsley, chopped, to serve

INSTRUCTIONS

1. Assemble, measure, and prepare the ingredients.
2. Cook the spaghetti according to package instructions.
3. Meanwhile, in a pan, cook the pancetta over a medium heat until crispy (4-8 mins, no need for extra oil as the pork will release its own fat). Remove from the pan and set aside.
4. In the same pan, add the garlic and cook until fragrant (about 30 seconds in the hot fat, make sure you don't burn it). Remove from heat.
5. In a bowl, whisk together the eggs, Parmesan cheese (reserve a little for serving), and a pinch of salt and pepper.
6. Once the pasta is cooked (retaining a little bite), drain in a colander, reserving 1 cup of pasta water.
7. Quickly transfer the hot pasta back to its hot pan (keep off the heat) and stir in the cooked garlic, cooked pancetta/lardons, and the egg mixture. Stir continuously so that the residual heat of the pasta and pan slowly cooks the sauce without scrambling the egg (if you left it too long and the pasta is too cool to cook the egg mix you can place it on a very low heat and stir like mad).
8. Add a little pasta water if the pasta seems too dry. Serve the pasta by using a large fork and tablespoon to twirl the pasta into domes and garnish with some extra grated Parmesan cheese, freshly ground black pepper, and parsley.

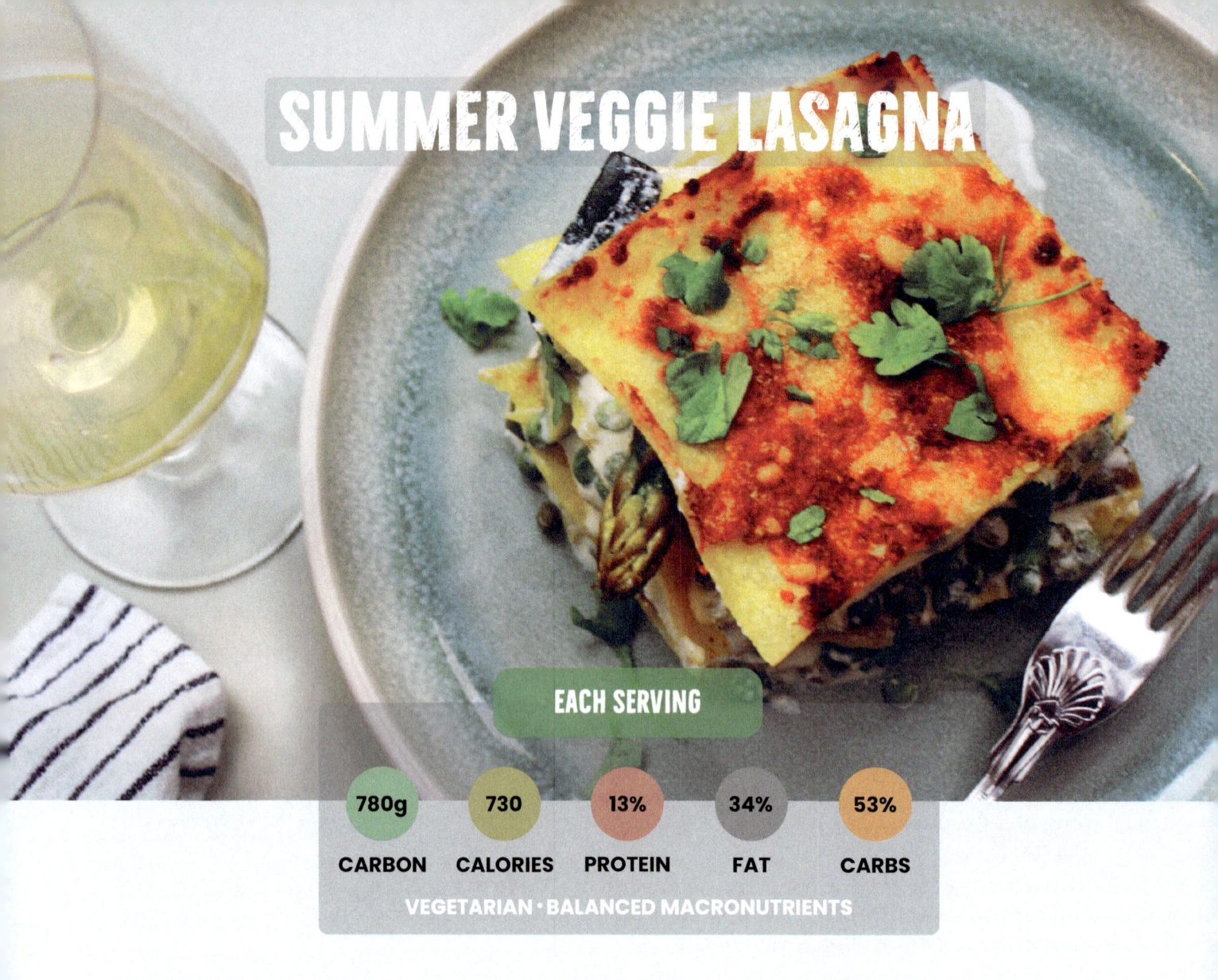

SUMMER VEGGIE LASAGNA

EACH SERVING

780g	730	13%	34%	53%
CARBON	CALORIES	PROTEIN	FAT	CARBS

VEGETARIAN • BALANCED MACRONUTRIENTS

Serves: 4   Prep Time: 15 mins   Cooking Time: 15 mins

LASAGNA just lighter and full of fresh veggies. This summer veggie lasagna is made with fresh asparagus, vibrant veggies, and zingy citrus and mint flavors balanced with a rich ricotta sauce. Great for long lunches and warm summer evenings.

CLIMATE KITCHEN HACKS traditional beef lasagna has a very large carbon footprint, is high in calories and contains lots of saturated fat. Try switching to this veggie version which is zesty, light, quicker to cook and an all round people pleaser. The same serving size has an 85% lower carbon footprint, 40% fewer calories, and 54% less fat than traditional beef lasagna.

Perfect Pastas

INGREDIENTS

- 4 sprays of canola (rapeseed) oil
- 2 cloves of garlic, minced/crushed
- 2 cups (240g) asparagus, trimmed and cut into thirds
- 2 cups (240g) zucchini/courgettes, halved then sliced lengthways
- 1 cup (240ml) of white wine
- 2 cups (240g) frozen peas
- 1 lemon, juice and zest
- 1 cup (240ml) double/whipping cream
- 1 cup (240g) of ricotta cheese
- 2 tbsp of fresh mint leaves, chopped
- Salt and pepper, to taste
- 8-10 sheets of fresh lasagna (300g)
- 1/4 cup (25g) of grated Parmesan cheese
- 9x9 inch / 23 x 23cm oven proof dish (or equivalent)

INSTRUCTIONS

1. Assemble, measure, and prepare the ingredients.
2. Preheat the fan assisted oven to 355°F / 180°C / Gas mark 4 (for a non-fan oven 400°F / 200°C / Gas mark 5).
3. In a large frying pan, heat the oil over a medium heat. Add the garlic and cook until softened (30 seconds). Add the asparagus and zucchini/courgettes and fry for another 2-4 minutes until the vegetables are just starting to go golden around the edges but still raw. Add the wine and cook for another 1-2 minutes.
4. Next, turn the heat to low and add the frozen peas, lemon zest, and cream (in that order - the peas cool the mix). Turn off the heat and mix in the ricotta cheese and chopped mint. Season with salt and pepper to taste.
5. In a baking dish, spread a thin layer of the sauce on the bottom. Place a layer of lasagna sheets over the sauce. Spread a layer of the sauce over the lasagna sheets. Repeat the layers until you reach the top of the dish or run out of sauce, making sure to finish with a layer of sauce (with no veggies) to cover the pasta.
6. Sprinkle the grated Parmesan cheese over the top and spray with a little olive oil to ensure an even crispy, golden crust. Place in the oven and bake for 15 minutes until the cheese on top is golden.
7. Serve up your delicious, zesty veggie lasagna.

TUNA PASTA BAKE WITH A PARMESAN CRUNCH

EACH SERVING

790g	500	26%	15%	59%
CARBON	CALORIES	PROTEIN	FAT	CARBS

LOW IN SATURATED FAT • LOW FAT • LOW CALORIE

Serves: 4   Prep Time: 15 mins   Cooking Time: 30 mins

TUNA PASTA BAKE will never be the same again. We have taken this weeknight staple to the next level with a tasty Parmesan crunch, tangy tomato sauce, and layers of soft then crispy penne pasta.

CLIMATE KITCHEN HACKS we switch grated cheese and cream for tomatoes and add a deliciously crunchy parmesan layer on top to deliver a bang of flavor with less dairy. The same serving size has a 45% lower carbon footprint, 40% fewer calories, and 80% less fat than traditional creamy tuna bake recipes.

INGREDIENTS

- 11 oz (320g) of pasta (penne works best)
- 1 onion (1 cup, 200g), finely diced
- 2 cloves of garlic, minced/crushed
- 2 cans of tomatoes (800g total weight), 1 plum and 1 chopped works well
- 1 small can sweetcorn (120g drained weight), drained
- 2 tsp of dried basil
- 2 cans (240g drained weight) skipjack tuna in brine (handline, pole-and-line, or troll caught)
- Salt and pepper, to taste
- 1/2 cup (50g) of Parmesan cheese, grated
- 8 sprays olive oil
- 11 x 11 inch / 22 x 22 cm deep baking dish/tray (or equivalent)

INSTRUCTIONS

1. Assemble, measure, and prepare the ingredients.
2. Preheat the fan assisted oven to 355°F / 180°C / Gas mark 4 (for a non-fan oven 400°F / 200°C / Gas mark 5).
3. Cook the pasta according to package instructions so it still has a little bite (al dente), drain, and reserve. Coat the cooked pasta with one spray of olive oil to stop it sticking together.
4. Meanwhile, take another saucepan, spray to coat with oil, and place on a medium heat. Add the onion and cook until softened (2-3 mins), then add the garlic and fry for another 30 seconds.
5. Stir in the canned tomatoes, sweetcorn, dried basil, and drained tuna. Season with salt and pepper to taste. Bring the mixture to a simmer and cook for a few minutes until the sauce is thickened.
6. Add the cooked pasta to the sauce and toss to coat. Transfer the coated pasta to an oven proof baking dish/tray. The dish must be large enough so that the pasta is just 2 pasta pieces deep. This allows the top layer of pasta to crisp up and the bottom layer stays soft adding delicious texture to the dish.
7. Shake to level off the pasta and sprinkle a good layer of grated Parmesan cheese evenly over the top. Spray to coat with olive oil to help evenly distribute the heat and create a crunchy, golden crust.
8. Bake in the hot oven for 20-25 minutes until the top is golden brown (don't worry about a few burnt ends they add crunch).
9. Let it cool down for a few minutes before serving.

PASTA PUTTANESCA

EACH SERVING

410g	430	14%	15%	71%
CARBON	CALORIES	PROTEIN	FAT	CARBS

LOW CALORIE • LOW IN SATURATED FAT • LOW FAT
VEGAN OPTION

Serves: 4   Prep Time: 10 mins   Cooking Time: 15 mins

PUTTANESCA sauce originated in Naples, Italy. It's made from tomatoes, olives, and capers which gives the dish a delightfully salty and tangy taste that leaves you wanting more. It's quick and easy to prepare and makes a great weeknight dish.

CLIMATE KITCHEN HACKS pasta puttanesca is a classic Italian dish that also has a low carbon footprint and a great nutritional balance. Go easy on the oil and this dish has 10% fewer calories and 40% less fat than traditional recipes.

INGREDIENTS

- 3/4 lb (340g) dry pasta (spaghetti, linguine or fettuccine / vegan option)
- 4 sprays of canola (rapeseed) oil
- 2 cloves of garlic, minced
- 4 anchovy fillets (30g), chopped
- 2 cans (28 oz/800g) of crushed/chopped tomatoes
- 1/2 cup (120g) of kalamata/black olives, pitted and chopped
- 1/4 cup (60g) of capers, drained
- 2 tsp of dried oregano
- Salt and pepper, to taste
- 2 tbsp Parmesan cheese, to serve (optional)
- 2 tbsp parsley, chopped, to serve

INSTRUCTIONS

1. Assemble, measure, and prepare the ingredients.
2. Cook the pasta according to package instructions, drain, and reserve. Coat the cooked pasta with one spray of olive oil to stop it sticking together.
3. Meanwhile, in a saucepan, heat the oil over low-medium heat. Add the garlic and anchovies and cook until fragrant (1 minute). Stir in the crushed tomatoes, olives, capers, oregano and bring the mixture to a simmer.
4. Season with salt and pepper to taste. Let the sauce simmer for at least 10 minutes, or until thickened.
5. Add half the sauce to the cooked pasta and toss to coat. Serve the pasta by using a large fork and tablespoon to twirl the pasta into domes.
6. Serve hot, topped with the remaining sauce, and garnished with some grated Parmesan cheese and fresh parsley.

PASTA ALLA NORMA

EACH SERVING

590g	500	13%	23%	64%
CARBON	CALORIES	PROTEIN	FAT	CARBS

LOW IN SATURATED FAT • BALANCED MACRONUTRIENTS
VEGETARIAN

Serves: 4　　Prep Time: 15 mins　　Cooking Time: 30 mins

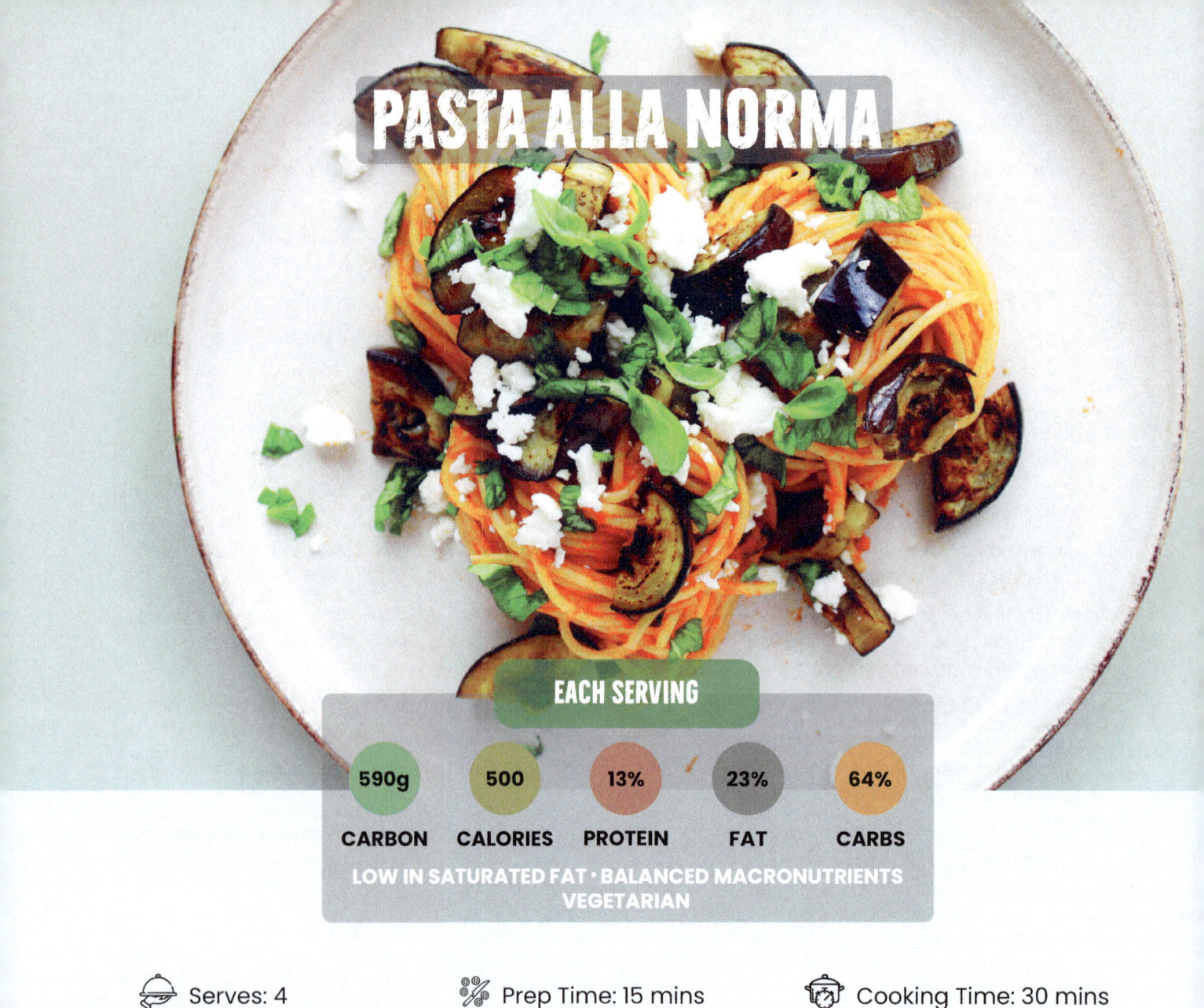

PASTA ALLA NORMA is a Sicilian favorite which is reportedly named after Bellini's famous opera "Norma" – an expression used to compliment the extraordinary taste. Our version certainly doesn't disappoint with creamy, salty feta balanced against tangy eggplant, tomatoes, and basil.

CLIMATE KITCHEN HACKS the eggplant slices are usually shallow fried in olive oil in this recipe. Instead we spray canola oil more sparingly to achieve the same golden, caramelized eggplant without the emissions and saturated fat. The same serving size has a 10% lower carbon footprint, 30% fewer calories, and 70% less fat.

Perfect Pastas

INGREDIENTS

- 3/4 lb (340g) dry pasta (spaghetti or linguine)
- 16 sprays canola (rapeseed) oil
- 2 eggplant/aubergine (4 cups, 500g), thick sliced and quartered
- 4 cloves of garlic, minced /crushed
- 3 cups (720g) of tomato sauce / passata (sieved tomatoes in a can)
- 4 tbsp of fresh basil, chopped
- 1 lemon, freshly squeezed
- Salt and pepper, to taste
- 1 cup (100g) of feta, crumbled

INSTRUCTIONS

1. Assemble, measure, and prepare the ingredients.
2. Cook the spaghetti according to package instructions, drain, and reserve. Coat the cooked pasta with one spray of olive oil to stop it sticking together.
3. Meanwhile, spray oil into a frying pan or skillet to coat and place on a medium-high heat. Spray the sliced eggplant with oil, arrange on the hot pan nicely spaced (you will need to do multiple batches), and fry until golden brown on both sides - use more oil as required. Once each batch is cooked, remove from the pan, and set aside.
4. In the same pan, add the garlic and cook until fragrant (30 seconds).
5. Add the tomato sauce to the pan and bring to a simmer.
6. Stir in half the fresh basil (2 tbsp) and lemon juice, season with salt and pepper to taste. Let it warm for a few minutes. Add the cooked pasta to the sauce and toss to coat.
7. Serve the pasta by using a large fork and tablespoon to twirl the pasta into domes.
8. Serve hot, topped with the fried eggplant slices, crumbled feta, and the remaining fresh basil.

SMOKY PORK CHILI

EACH SERVING

800g	710	27%	23%	50%
CARBON	CALORIES	PROTEIN	FAT	CARBS

Serves: 4   Prep Time: 15 mins   Cooking Time: 30 mins

CHILI CON CARNE is the official dish of the US state of Texas as designated by law. The legislation states that "One cannot be a true son or daughter of the state without having his taste buds tingle at the thought of the treat that is real, honest-to-goodness, unadulterated Texas chili". Our pork chili certainly passes the Texas taste test with the smoky flavors of pancetta and paprika, the tang of balsamic and herbs, balanced by earthy beetroot and rich pork.

CLIMATE KITCHEN HACKS we switch beef mince for pork mince and halve the amount of meat used by replacing it with flavorful black or pinto beans. We add grated beetroot to give color, texture, and depth of flavor to the pork, and a sprinkling of Parmesan (rather than masses of grated soft cheese) provides that flavorful cheesy punch without the saturated fat. The same serving size has a 90% lower carbon footprint, 20% fewer calories, and 50% less fat than beef-based recipes.

INGREDIENTS

- 1/2 cup (120g) of diced pancetta or pork lardons
- 1 lb (300g) of ground/minced pork
- 1/2 cup (120g) beet(root), grated
- 4 sprays canola (rapeseed) oil
- 1 onion (1/2 cup / 150g), diced
- 3 cloves of garlic, minced/crushed
- 2-4 tsp of mild chili powder (1-2 tsp if hot chili powder)
- 1 tsp of ground cumin
- 2 tsp of smoked paprika
- 1 tsp of dried oregano
- 1 tbsp balsamic vinegar
- 1 tsp light brown sugar
- 1 can (14oz/400g) of diced tomatoes
- 1 can (14oz/400g) of kidney beans, drained and rinsed
- 1 can (14oz/400g) of black beans or pinto beans, drained and rinsed
- Salt and pepper, to taste
- 1 cup (240g) dry rice
- 1/4 cup (25g) Parmesan, finely grated
- 4 tbsp (60g) sour cream

INSTRUCTIONS

1. Assemble, measure, and prepare the ingredients. Use mild chili if you don't like too much heat, 2 tsp for a warm chili, 3 tsp for a kick, and 4 tsp for some heat. If you like it spicy use 1-2 tsp of hot chili powder.
2. Take a large skillet or Dutch oven, heat on medium-high and add the diced pancetta/lardons. Fry for 2-3 minutes until starting to crisp and release their fat then add the grated beetroot and ground/minced pork and fry until the mince starts to brown (another 4-6 minutes). Remove the meat and beet from the pan and reserve in a separate bowl.
3. Add the onion to the pan (spray with a little oil if required) and cook until softened (2-3 minutes), add the garlic and fry for another 30 seconds.
4. Stir in the chili powder, cumin, smoked paprika, and oregano. Add the balsamic vinegar, light brown sugar, diced tomatoes, kidney beans, pinto/black beans plus the browned pancetta, mince, and beetroot. Bring to a simmer.
5. Season with a pinch of salt and pepper. Add a little water if the chili needs loosening. Let the chili simmer for at least 30 minutes (lid partially on), to allow the flavors to infuse.
6. Meanwhile, cook rice according to package instructions.
7. Taste, adjust the seasoning if necessary, and serve the hot chili over the rice, garnishing with grated Parmesan cheese and sour cream.

CRISPY CRUMB CASSOULET

EACH SERVING

| 600g | 740 | 18% | 52% | 30% |
| CARBON | CALORIES | PROTEIN | FAT | CARBS |

Serves: 4   Prep Time: 15 mins   Cooking Time: 45 mins

CASSOULET is a classic French dish purportedly created during the Hundred Years War in the 14th Century. The story goes that the townspeople of Castelnaudary in Southern France were under siege from the English and running low on supplies. They gathered what they had left and cooked up the first cassoulet, a dish so hearty it spurred them on to push the English hordes back to the sea. Although almost certainly historically inaccurate, it's a creation myth befitting this delicious dish. Our version is comforting, moreish, and tangy - the ultimate comfort food to help fight-off marauding hordes or maybe just the winter sniffles.

CLIMATE KITCHEN HACKS sausage cassoulet is a variation of the traditional French dish. In this version, sausages are used instead of the traditional meats like duck or mutton. Helping to reduce the carbon footprint by 80%.

Winter Warmers

INGREDIENTS

- 1 lb (450g) sausages, whole or cut into bite-sized pieces
- 4 sprays canola (rapeseed) oil
- 1 onion (1 cup, 150g), diced
- 2 cloves of garlic, minced/crushed
- 2 cups (240g) carrots, sliced lengthways (no need to peel)
- 1 cup (240g) celery, sliced
- 1 can (0.9lb, 400g) plum tomatoes
- 1 can (0.9lb, 400g) white beans/cannellini/white kidney beans, drained and rinsed
- 1 cup (240ml) vegetable stock
- 1 tsp dried thyme
- 2-3 sprigs fresh rosemary, finely chopped
- 1 tsp mustard powder
- Salt and pepper, to taste
- 1 cup (100g) panko breadcrumbs
- 1/4 cup (60ml) olive oil

INSTRUCTIONS

1. Assemble, measure, and prepare the ingredients.
2. Preheat a fan oven to 390ºF / 200ºC / Gas mark 6 (for a non-fan oven 425ºF / 220ºC / Gas mark 7).
3. In a heavy frying pan or skillet, fry the sausages over a medium-high heat until browned on all sides (spray a little oil if required), set aside.
4. Place a Dutch oven or casserole dish on a medium heat, coat with 2-3 sprays of oil and add the diced onion, cook until softened (2-3 mins), add the garlic and fry for another 30 seconds.
5. Add the carrots, celery, and tomatoes, and stir well.
6. Add the drained white beans and the cooked sausages to the pot.
7. Add enough of the vegetable stock to just cover the ingredients.
8. Add thyme, rosemary, mustard, and a pinch of salt & pepper.
9. Bring to a simmer and cover with a lid, transfer to the preheated oven. Cook for 30 mins.
10. Meanwhile mix the breadcrumbs and olive oil in a bowl, after the cassoulet has cooked for 30 mins, remove from the oven, and spread the oiled breadcrumbs over the surface.
11. Leave the lid off and return the cassoulet to the oven and bake for an additional 10-15 minutes until the breadcrumbs are golden brown and crispy.

CHICKEN, LEEK, AND SWEET POTATO PIE

EACH SERVING

480g	780	20%	41%	39%
CARBON	CALORIES	PROTEIN	FAT	CARBS

Serves: 4   Prep Time: 30 mins   Cooking Time: 40 mins

THE MIGHTY PIE is certainly a classic dish and we have the Romans to thank for inventing it, a sumptuous combination of buttery pastry stuffed with rich meat. The English went on to develop humble pie. Enjoyed by peasant folk, it consisted of pastry stuffed with 'umbles', which were the unwanted cuts of cheap meat! Our pie recipe is fit for kings and peasants alike, with tasty chicken, sweet potato, and salty melt-in-the-mouth pastry.

CLIMATE KITCHEN HACKS we use chicken thighs rather than chicken breast, and replace some chicken with sweet potato for a greater depth of flavor and lower carbon footprint (the high demand for chicken breast creates waste in other cuts). We use a thinner, crispier pastry to save on dairy and saturated fat. The same serving size has a 30% lower carbon footprint and 20% less fat.

Winter Warmers

INGREDIENTS

For the filling:
- 2 sweet potatoes (400g), peeled but whole
- 8 sprays canola (rapeseed) oil
- 1 lb (450g) boneless, skinless chicken thighs, cut into bite-sized pieces
- 1 onion (1 cup, 150g), diced
- 2 cloves of garlic, minced/crushed
- 2 leeks (300g), sliced
- 1 cup (240ml) chicken broth/stock
- 1/2 cup (120g) heavy cream
- 1 tsp dried thyme
- 1 tbsp mustard
- 1/2 tsp celery salt
- Salt and pepper, to taste
- 3 tbsp cornstarch mixed with 5 tbsp cold water

For the short crust pastry (this pastry is super easy, but use shop bought if you prefer):
- 1 1/2 cups (180g) all-purpose flour
- 1 tsp salt
- 1/3 cup (80g) unsalted butter, cold and diced
- 1/6 cup (40ml) ice water

- 8x8 inch / 20x20 cm pie dish or oven proof dish

INSTRUCTIONS

1. Assemble, measure, and prepare the ingredients. Preheat a fan oven to 375ºF / 190ºC / Gas mark 5 (for a non-fan oven 410ºF / 210ºC / Gas mark 6).
2. Place the peeled sweet potatoes on a plate and microwave for 4-5 minutes (800W power) until nearly (but not quite) cooked through (a knife should pierce to the center of the potatoes easily). Allow to cool and cut into 1 cm / ½ inch cubes.
3. Meanwhile to make the filling, heat a large pot, skillet, or Dutch oven over a high heat with a few sprays of oil. Add the chicken and cook for about 4-6 minutes until lightly browned. Remove the chicken from the pan and set it aside.
4. Add the onion to the pan and cook until softened (2-3 mins), add the garlic and fry for another 30 seconds. Add the sliced leeks and cook for an additional 2-3 minutes, until softened. Add the stock, cream, thyme, mustard, celery salt, and a pinch of salt & pepper, and bring the mixture to a gentle simmer.
5. Slowly add the cornstarch-water mix, 2 tbsp at a time, stirring constantly, until the sauce thickens to a thin cream like consistency (you may not need all the cornstarch mix). Return the browned chicken to the pot, add the sweet potato cubes, and stir well to combine. Turn the heat to low and allow the mixture to thicken for 10 minutes whilst you prepare the pastry.
6. To make the pastry crust, take a large bowl and mix the flour and salt together. Using a pastry cutter or your fingertips, cut/crumble the butter into the flour mixture until it resembles coarse crumbs. The key is to keep the mix as cool as possible so use just fingertips and don't worry if there are still some small buttery lumps.
7. Next, gradually add the ice water to the pastry mix, 1 tbsp at a time, until the dough comes together. Knead very gently a few times to fully incorporate the ingredients.
8. Roll out the dough on a cool floured surface (keep flouring the surface of the dough as you roll it out to stop it sticking) to a size just bigger than the oven proof dish. Taste and season the chicken filling. Pour into the oven proof dish.
9. Cover the dish with the pastry layer and press the pastry to the edges of the dish with the back of a fork to seal. Trim away the excess pastry (you can make a design for the top of the pie to avoid wasting the pastry). Poke a few holes in the middle of the pie with a sharp knife to allow the steam to escape. Brush the top with a little milk to give that glazed look in the finished pie.
10. Bake the pie for 30-35 minutes until the crust is golden brown and the filling is hot and bubbly.

AROMATIC VEGETABLE TAGINE

EACH SERVING

540g	550	9%	13%	78%
CARBON	CALORIES	PROTEIN	FAT	CARBS

LOW FAT • LOW IN SATURATED FAT • LOW CALORIE
VEGAN OPTION

Serves: 4   Prep Time: 25 mins   Cooking Time: 25 mins

A TAGINE is both a cooking vessel and a famous dish which was supposedly invented by the nomadic Berbers of Northwest Africa who used the conical-shaped earthenware pots as portable ovens. Our recipe, that can be made in a tagine or a regular pot, captures all the delicate aromatic flavors of Morocco which combine perfectly with the caramelized veggies and nutty couscous.

CLIMATE KITCHEN HACKS tagine is packed full of so much flavor we don't think it needs meat. In this recipe we switch out the traditional lamb for delicious flavor absorbing root vegetables like carrots, parsnips, and sweet potato. The same serving size has a 90% lower carbon footprint, 40% fewer calories, and 80% less fat than lamb tagine.

INGREDIENTS

- 8 sprays canola (rapeseed) oil
- 2-3 carrots (1 cup, 240g), cut into batons (no need to peel)
- 2-3 parsnips (1 cup, 240g), cut into batons (no need to peel)
- 1 large sweet potato (1 cup, 240g), peeled and cubed
- 2-3 red onion (1 ½ cup, 360g), finely chopped
- 4 cloves of garlic, minced
- 1 tsp of ground ginger / or 1 tbsp fresh ginger finely chopped or grated
- 1 tsp of ground cumin
- 1/2 tsp of ground cinnamon
- 1/2 tsp of ground black pepper
- 1/2 tsp of saffron strands (optional)
- 1 cup (240ml) of vegetable broth/stock
- 1 can (400g) of diced tomatoes
- 1 cup (240g) of dried apricots, quartered
- 2-3 red and yellow peppers (2 cup, 340g), sliced or quartered
- Salt to taste
- 1 cup (240g) couscous
- 1 tbsp olive oil
- 4 tbsp pine nuts, to serve (optional)
- 1/4 cup of chopped fresh cilantro/coriander or parsley for garnish
- Tagine or Dutch oven dish

INSTRUCTIONS

1. Preheat a fan oven to 430°F / 220°C / Gas mark 7 (for a non-fan oven 465°F / 240°C / Gas mark 8).
2. Assemble, measure, and prepare the ingredients. Saffron is optional as it is expensive and can be difficult to source - it adds a floral/aromatic flavor to the dish which some love and others don't!
3. Begin by spraying oil to cover a baking tray and add the carrots, parsnips, and sweet potato. Spray the top of the vegetables with more oil and cook in the oven for 15 minutes until the edges of the vegetables start to caramelize.
4. Meanwhile, spray coat oil in the tagine or Dutch oven and place over a medium heat on the hob. Add the onion and cook for 2-3 minutes until softened, add the garlic for another 30 seconds.
5. Next, stir in the ginger, cumin, cinnamon, black pepper, and saffron. Cook for another 1-2 minutes or until fragrant. Stir in the broth/stock, diced tomatoes, apricots, peppers, pre-roasted vegetables, and a pinch of salt. Bring to a simmer.
6. Reduce the heat to low and cover the tagine or pan. Cook for 15-20 minutes to let the vegetables absorb the flavors.
7. Meanwhile, mix 1 tbsp of olive oil into the dry couscous in a heat proof bowl, pour 300ml of boiling water over the couscous, cover and let cook for 5-10 minutes.
8. Whilst the couscous cooks, toast the pine nuts (if using) by placing them in a dry pan over a medium heat for 5 minutes until they start to turn brown (keep a careful eye on the pan as it is easy to burn the nuts). Remove from the pan and roughly chop the nuts.
9. Fluff the couscous with a fork, season with salt to taste, and mix through half the chopped pine nuts and half the chopped coriander/cilantro, plus extra oil if required.
10. Serve the tagine with coriander/cilantro and pine nuts to garnish and accompanied by the finished couscous.

LIGHTER MOUSSAKA

EACH SERVING

800g	560	25%	50%	25%
CARBON	CALORIES	PROTEIN	FAT	CARBS

Serves: 6   Prep Time: 30 mins   Cooking Time: 30 mins

MOUSSAKA takes its name from the Arabic word musaqqa'ah which means chilled, because the dish can be eaten hot or cold. We have taken Moussaka back to its original recipe and we make it with ground pork rather than lamb or beef. The sweet pork and cinnamon are perfectly balanced by the salty eggplant, and creamy oat-based béchamel sauce. Creating a lighter, less oily moussaka which makes a perfect lunch or dinner.

CLIMATE KITCHEN HACKS we use pork rather than lamb or beef. We switch cream/cheese for an oatmilk bechamel sauce and we oven bake the eggplant rather than deep frying. Saving on carbon emissions and saturated fat. The same serving size has a 75% lower carbon footprint, 40% fewer calories, and 50% less fat than lamb and cream-based Moussaka.

Winter Warmers

INGREDIENTS

- 3 lbs (1.3kg) of eggplant/aubergine, sliced into 1/4-inch (6mm) rounds
- 12 sprays canola (rapeseed) oil
- 1 lb (450g) of ground/minced pork
- 1 large onion (240g), finely chopped
- 4 cloves of garlic, minced/crushed
- 2 cans (each 14oz/400g) of diced tomatoes
- 2 tsp of dried oregano
- 1/2 tsp of ground cinnamon
- Salt and pepper to taste
- 1/2 cup of chopped fresh parsley

For the béchamel sauce:

- 3 cups (720ml) of oat milk
- 2 tbsp (30g) of butter
- 1/4 cup (30g) of all-purpose flour
- Salt and pepper to taste
- 3 eggs, lightly beaten
- 1 cup (100g) of grated Parmesan cheese
- Oven dish 12x12 inch / 30x30 cm (or equivalent)

INSTRUCTIONS

1. First slice the eggplant/aubergine and place in a colander, sprinkle with salt and let sit for 30 minutes to release the bitterness. Preheat the fan oven to 430°F / 220°C / Gas mark 7 (for a non-fan oven 465°F / 240°C / Gas mark 8).
2. Assemble, measure, and prepare the remainder of the ingredients.
3. Rinse and dry the eggplant/aubergine slices, spray oil onto a couple of baking trays to coat and arrange the slices in a single layer. Spray a little more oil over the top of the eggplant/aubergine and place in the oven for 20 minutes (turning halfway and spraying with a little more oil).
4. Meanwhile, take a skillet or frying pan, spray with oil to coat, and place on a medium heat. Add the ground pork and cook for about 4-6 minutes until browned. Drain any excess fat.
5. To the meat, add the onion and gentle fry for 2-3 minutes, add the garlic for 30 seconds, then add the diced tomatoes, oregano, cinnamon, salt, pepper, and parsley. Simmer for 10-15 minutes or until the meat sauce thickens. Whilst the pork sauce thickens, take another pan, and gently heat the oat milk until it starts to steam - keep warm.
6. In a third saucepan start preparing the béchamel sauce by melting the butter over a medium heat. Whisk in the flour and cook for 1-2 minutes or until the mixture becomes smooth, bubbly and turns a slightly darker color. Slowly whisk in the hot milk 1 tbsp at a time. Stir constantly - the mix will at first solidify to a wallpaper paste consistency, then as you add more milk it will form a thin custard texture. If the mixture splits (the liquid and solids separate) you can sprinkle in a little more flour and stir like mad to try and save the sauce. Bring to a gentle simmer and cook for 2-3 minutes or until the sauce thickens. Season with a pinch of salt & pepper.
7. Remove the sauce from the heat and whisk in the beaten eggs and a ½ cup of Parmesan cheese, keep stirring constantly. Once the béchamel sauce is done, the eggplant/aubergines are caramelized in the oven, and pork sauce has thickened, you are ready to assemble the moussaka.
8. Start by spreading half of the meat sauce in the bottom of the oven dish. Arrange the eggplant slices on top of the meat sauce. Spread the remaining meat sauce over the eggplant. Pour the béchamel sauce over the top of the eggplant and meat mixture. Sprinkle the remaining ½ cup of grated Parmesan cheese over the top.
9. Bake the moussaka for about 30 minutes until the top is golden brown and the sauce is bubbly.
10. Let it cool for 10-15 minutes before slicing and serving.

CHICKEN TIKKA MASALA

EACH SERVING

800g	650	29%	25%	46%
CARBON	CALORIES	PROTEIN	FAT	CARBS

Serves: 4

Prep Time: 20 mins

Marinate Time: 60 mins

Cooking Time: 40 mins

CHICKEN TIKKA MASALA was purportedly invented in Glasgow, Scotland in the 1970s when a Bangladeshi chef added cream and tomatoes to his hot chicken tikka to please a spice averse customer. Our recipe is sure to please any diner with spicy chicken and tangy fresh tomatoes wrapped up in a velvety rich sauce.

CLIMATE KITCHEN HACKS we switch the dairy cream for plain yogurt and add a tablespoon of rich cashew butter to lower the carbon footprint and fat whilst maintaining the silky, rich masala sauce. The same serving size has a 10% lower carbon footprint, 15% fewer calories, and 50% less fat than cream-based chicken tikka masala.

Classic Curries

INGREDIENTS

- 1 tbsp of grated ginger
- 2 cloves of garlic, minced/crushed
- 1 tsp of ground cumin
- 1 tsp of ground coriander
- 1/2 tsp of ground turmeric
- 1/2 tsp of ground cayenne pepper
- Salt and pepper to taste
- 2 cups (500ml) of plain/natural yogurt
- 1 lb (450g) of boneless, skinless chicken breast, cut into 1-inch (2.5cm) cubes
- 8 sprays canola (rapeseed) oil
- 1 onion (1 cup, 150g), finely chopped
- 6 fresh tomatoes (3 cups, 480g), diced and rinsed in a colander to remove the seeds
- 1 tbsp smooth cashew butter
- 1 cup (240ml) of chicken broth/stock
- 1 1/2 cups (250g) rice, dry
- 1/4 cup of chopped fresh cilantro/coriander
- 4 skewers for cooking the chicken (if wooden soak in water for 30 mins before using)
- Food processor or handheld blender

INSTRUCTIONS

1. Assemble, measure, and prepare the ingredients. Use 1/2 tsp of cayenne for warmth, 1 tsp for a hot kick, and more than 1 tsp for a spicy curry - remember you can always taste and add more later.
2. In a large bowl, mix the ginger, garlic, cumin, coriander, turmeric, cayenne pepper, a pinch of salt & pepper, and half the yogurt (1 cup). Add the chicken and mix well to coat. Cover and refrigerate for at least 1 hour or ideally overnight.
3. Once the chicken has marinated, thread the pieces onto skewers and grill or broil for 10-15 minutes, turning as each side browns, until cooked through.
4. Meanwhile, spray coat the oil in a large skillet or saucepan over a medium heat. Add the onion and cook until softened (2-3 minutes).
5. Add the diced tomatoes, turn the heat to low and simmer for 10 minutes to soften the tomatoes.
6. Stir in the cashew butter, half the broth/stock (1/2 a cup), and the remaining half of the yogurt (1 cup). Bring the mixture to a simmer, cover, and leave on a low heat.
7. Cook rice according to package instructions.
8. Take the onion and tomato sauce and blitz using a blender (handheld is easiest). Pulse until smooth and for an even smoother sauce you can push the blended mix through a sieve using the back of a spoon.
9. Transfer the smooth sauce to a clean pan and add the chicken from the skewers to the sauce. Simmer for 5-7 minutes to let the chicken absorb the flavors. Use the remaining stock to achieve your desired curry consistency.
10. Finally, stir through half the cilantro, serve over the rice, and garnish the curry with the remaining cilantro/coriander and some chopped tomatoes.

KORMA CURRY

EACH SERVING

700g	615	27%	27%	46%
CARBON	CALORIES	PROTEIN	FAT	CARBS

Serves: 4   Prep Time: 20 mins   Cooking Time: 40 mins

KORMA CURRY was originally considered a showy banquet dish that used expensive flavorings like saffron, cardamon, and nutmeg. It was a firm favorite of the fifth Mughal emperor who was known as the king of the world. With tangy chicken, vibrant ginger and silky-smooth sauce, we think our korma is certainly fit for a king.

CLIMATE KITCHEN HACKS we switch the cream for coconut yogurt plus a tablespoon of rich cashew butter to lower the carbon footprint and fat whilst maintaining the silky, rich korma sauce - a sauce traditionally made with ground nuts. The same serving size has a 10% lower carbon footprint, 10% fewer calories, and 35% less fat than cream-based chicken korma.

INGREDIENTS

- 12 sprays canola (rapeseed) oil
- 1 onion (1 cup, 240g), finely chopped
- 1 tbsp of fresh ginger, finely chopped or grated
- 2 cloves of garlic, minced/crushed
- 2 tsp of ground cumin
- 2 tsp of ground coriander
- 1 tsp of ground turmeric
- 1/2 tsp of ground cinnamon
- 1/2 tsp of ground cardamon
- Salt and pepper, to taste
- 1 lb (450g) of boneless chicken breast, cut into 1-inch (2.5cm) cubes
- 1 cup (240ml) of coconut yogurt
- 1 tbsp of smooth cashew butter (fairtrade certified)
- 1 cup (240ml) of chicken stock/broth
- 1 1/2 cups (250g) rice, dry
- 1/4 cup of chopped fresh cilantro/coriander
- Flaked almonds, toasted in a dry pan for a few minutes, to serve (optional)

INSTRUCTIONS

1. Assemble, measure, and prepare the ingredients.
2. Heat the oil in a large skillet or saucepan over a medium heat. Add the onion and cook until softened, about 2-3 minutes, add the ginger and fry for a further 1-2 minutes. Finally, add the garlic and fry for 30 seconds until fragrant.
3. Next, stir in the cumin, coriander, turmeric, cinnamon, cardamon, and a pinch of salt & pepper. Cook for 1-2 minutes or until fragrant.
4. Add the chicken and fry for about 4-5 minutes until browned on all sides (spray a little more oil if required to keep it sizzling nicely).
5. Stir in the coconut yogurt (retain a little for serving), cashew butter, and half the stock (1/2 cup). Bring the mixture to a simmer.
6. Reduce the heat to low, cover and simmer for 25 minutes, until the chicken is tender.
7. Whilst the curry simmers, cook rice according to package instructions.
8. Once the curry is cooked through, taste and season with salt and pepper, and add extra stock until the desired curry consistency is reached.
9. Finally, stir through half the cilantro, and serve over the rice. Garnish the curry with the remaining cilantro/coriander, extra yogurt, and flaked almonds (optional)
10. Enjoy your creamy korma - fit for the king of the world.

CAULIFLOWER & COCONUT JALFREZI

EACH SERVING

610g	500	13%	10%	77%
CARBON	CALORIES	PROTEIN	FAT	CARBS

LOW CALORIE • LOW FAT • LOW IN SATURATED FAT
VEGAN OPTION

Serves: 4   Prep Time: 20 mins   Cooking Time: 30 mins

JALFREZI means spicy-fry and was invented during the English occupation of India when many Indians were forced into poverty. Indian servants would often eat the leftovers from meals and banquets but would have to spice up the bland English fare with onion, spices, and ghee. Our jalfrezi recipe is meat free and one of our absolute favorite dishes – it's vibrant, warming, tangy, and super healthy.

CLIMATE KITCHEN HACKS we switch chicken for cauliflower & chickpea in this delicious jalfrezi recipe. The bold spice flavors absorb into the vegetables and create a sensational dish – we promise you won't miss the meat. The same serving size has a 50% lower carbon footprint, 45% fewer calories, and 80% less fat than chicken jalfrezi.

Classic Curries

INGREDIENTS

- 1 head of a cauliflower (800g), broken into florets
- 8 sprays canola (rapeseed) oil
- 2 red onion (2 cup, 300g), finely diced
- 2 cloves of garlic, minced/crushed
- 1 tbsp of fresh ginger, grated or finely diced
- 1 red bell pepper (1 cup, 240g), sliced
- 1 green bell pepper (1 cup, 240g), sliced
- 1 can (400g) chickpeas, rinsed and drained
- 2 tsp of ground cumin
- 2 tsp of ground coriander
- 1 tsp of ground turmeric
- 1/4 tsp of ground cayenne pepper
- Salt and pepper, to taste
- 1 can (14.5 oz/411g) of diced tomatoes
- 1 cup (240ml) vegetable stock/broth
- 1/2 cup (120g) coconut yogurt
- 1/4 cup (40g) of fresh cilantro/coriander, chopped
- 1 1/2 cups (250g) rice, dry
- 2 tbsp flaked almonds, to serve (optional)

INSTRUCTIONS

1. Assemble, measure, and prepare the ingredients. Use 1/4 tsp of cayenne for warmth, 1/2 tsp for a hot kick, and 1 or more for a very spicy curry - remember you can always taste and add more later.
2. Spray oil in a large skillet or wok to coat and heat over a medium-high heat. Add the onion and cook until softened, about 2-3 minutes. Add the ginger and cook for another 1-2 minutes, then the garlic for 30 seconds, until aromatic.
3. Stir in the cumin, coriander, turmeric, cayenne pepper, and a pinch of salt & pepper. Spray with a little more oil and cook for 1-2 minutes or until fragrant.
4. Stir in the diced tomatoes, cauliflower, and stock/broth. Bring the mixture to a simmer. Reduce the heat to low and cook for 10 minutes or until the sauce thickens (no lid).
5. Add the bell peppers and chickpeas, loosely cover the pan with a lid or chopping board (allows the steam to build and cook the vegetables but the steam then escapes to reduce and thicken the sauce). Simmer for a further 20 minutes.
6. Whilst the curry simmers, cook rice according to package instructions.
7. Once the curry is ready, stir in the yogurt and half the chopped cilantro/coriander. Serve the curry over the rice and garnish with the remaining cilantro/coriander, a little extra yogurt, and flaked almonds.

JAPANESE CURRY RICE

EACH SERVING

800g	740	20%	27%	53%
CARBON	CALORIES	PROTEIN	FAT	CARBS

BALANCED MACONUTRIENTS

Serves: 4   Prep Time: 20 mins   Cooking Time: 40 mins

JAPANESE CURRY RICE also known as "kare raisu" is a popular dish made with a roux-based curry sauce served over rice. This recipe is one big hug in a bowl - a comforting, mild, and sweet curry packed full of tender vegetables and tasty pork.

CLIMATE KITCHEN HACKS we make this dish with pork rather than beef. We spray don't drizzle the oil. The same serving size has an 85% lower carbon footprint, 10% fewer calories, and 25% less fat than traditional recipes.

Classic Curries

INGREDIENTS

- 1 1/2 cups (250g) of Japanese short grain rice, dry
- 8 sprays canola (rapeseed) oil
- 1 lb (450g) of pork filet/tenderloin, cut into 1-inch (2.5cm) cubes
- 1 large onion (1 cup, 240g), finely chopped
- 1 tbsp of fresh ginger, grated or finely diced
- 2 cloves of garlic, minced/crushed
- 2 carrots (1 cup, 240g), diced
- 2 cups baby/new potatoes (480g), diced
- 1 apple (1/2 cup, 120g), peeled and grated
- 2 cups (480ml) of chicken broth/stock
- 1 cup (240ml) of water
- 3 tbsp (45ml) of curry roux
- Salt and pepper, to taste
- Japanese pickles, to serve (optional)

INSTRUCTIONS

1. Assemble, measure, and prepare the ingredients.
2. Cook the Japanese rice following the guidelines on the packet, set aside once done.
3. Whilst the rice cooks, spray half the oil (4 sprays) to coat a skillet or heavy frying pan and place on the highest heat until smoking hot. Brown the pork cubes to sear the outside of the meat (no need to cook all the way through). Set aside.
4. In another large saucepan or frying pan, spray the remainder of the oil (4 sprays) to coat, and place on a medium heat. Add the onion and cook until softened, about 2-3 minutes. Add the ginger for another 1-2 minutes, then the garlic for 30 seconds, until fragrant.
5. Stir in the seared pork, carrot, potatoes, apple, broth, water, curry roux, and a pinch of salt & pepper. Bring the mixture to a simmer.
6. Reduce the heat to low and gently simmer for 30-40 minutes until the meat is cooked through, the vegetables are tender, and the sauce is a gravy consistency (add more water if it gets too dry/thick).
7. Taste, adjust seasoning if required, and serve the curry over the cooked rice with your favorite Japanese pickles.

CRISPY AUBERGINE KATSU CURRY

EACH SERVING

770g	755	12%	28%	60%
CARBON	CALORIES	PROTEIN	FAT	CARBS

BALANCED MACRONUTRIENTS • LOW IN SATURATED FAT
VEGAN OPTION

Serves: 4   Prep Time: 20 mins   Cooking Time: 30 mins

KATSU CURRY was originally known as 'Chiba-san's curry' named after a Tokyo Giants baseball player called Shigeru Chiba who supposedly first asked for his katsu (meat fried in breadcrumb) and Japanese curry to be served together. Our version is a no regrets veggie feast - the eggplant/aubergine stays so succulent inside its crispy coating and is smothered in a zingy, silky curry sauce. This katsu curry will leave your mouth watering whilst delivering a great balance of nutrients and is low in saturated fat.

CLIMATE KITCHEN HACKS we switch the meat for eggplant/aubergine, use reduced fat coconut milk, whilst going easy on the breadcrumbs and oil. The same serving size has a 40% lower carbon footprint, 40% fewer calories, and 55% less fat than traditional chicken katsu curry recipes.

Classic Curries

INGREDIENTS

- 4 aubergines/eggplant (900g), thick sliced (1cm / 1/2 inch thick)
- 1 tbsp salt
- 1/2 cup (60g) of all-purpose flour
- 2 large eggs, beaten (or egg substitute for vegan option)
- 1 1/2 cup (100g) of panko breadcrumbs
- 8 sprays of canola (rapeseed) oil
- 1.5-2 cups (250g) of Japanese rice, dry
- 1 large onion (1 cup, 240g), finely chopped
- 1 tbsp of fresh ginger, grated or finely diced
- 2 cloves of garlic, minced
- 2 tbsp of mild or medium curry powder
- 2 tsp garam masala
- 1 can (400g) reduced fat coconut milk
- 1 cup (240ml) of vegetable broth/stock
- Salt and pepper, to taste
- Pickles / gherkins, sliced, to serve, (optional)
- Wire rack for cooking

INSTRUCTIONS

1. Preheat a fan oven to 430°F / 220°C / Gas mark 7 with a large baking tray inside (for a non-fan oven 465°F / 240°C / Gas mark 8).
2. Slice the aubergine/eggplant and place in a colander, sprinkle generously with salt and leave for 5-10 minutes to remove the bitterness. Rinse in water and dry with soft kitchen paper or tea-towel once ready.
3. Whilst the aubergine/eggplant sits in the salt, assemble, measure, and prepare the other ingredients. Use mild or medium curry powder depending on how hot you want the sauce.
4. Cook the rice according to package instructions. Once cooked set aside to keep warm.
5. Meanwhile, place the flour, beaten eggs, and panko breadcrumbs into separate shallow bowls. Dredge the aubergine/eggplant in the flour, then the eggs, and finally coat with the panko breadcrumbs. Spray with oil to lightly coat.
6. Place the coated aubergine/eggplant slices on a large wire rack and place the rack on the hot baking sheet in the oven for 20 minutes until golden brown. The hot tray radiates heat to the underside of the aubergine/eggplant creating a super crispy outside with no need to turn through cooking.
7. As the aubergine/eggplant cooks, heat 4 sprays of oil in a frying pan or large saucepan over a medium-high heat. Add the onion and cook until softened, about 2-3 minutes. Add the ginger for another 1-2 minutes, and the garlic for a further 30 seconds. Stir in the curry powder and garam masala and cook for 1-2 minutes or until fragrant.
8. Stir in the coconut milk and broth/stock, bring to a simmer and cook for 10-15 minutes, until the sauce thickens. Season with salt and pepper, to taste.
9. Serve the curry sauce over the cooked rice and crispy aubergine/eggplant with the sliced pickles. Delicious.

CHICKEN RENDANG CURRY

EACH SERVING

780g	760	26%	42%	32%
CARBON	CALORIES	PROTEIN	FAT	CARBS

Serves: 4   Prep Time: 20 mins   Cooking Time: 100 mins

RENDANG is a dry curry dish from Indonesia, specifically from West Sumatra, made with meat cooked in a rich and complex spice paste and coconut milk. Our rendang recipe has succulent chicken packed full of Indonesian flavors and can be served dry or with extra sauce.

CLIMATE KITCHEN HACKS we make this dish with chicken thighs rather than beef to save on the carbon footprint. We use reduced fat coconut milk to save on the saturated fat. Then we add toasted coconut flakes to ramp the flavor. The same serving size has an 85% lower carbon footprint and 15% less fat than traditional beef-based recipes.

Classic Curries

INGREDIENTS

For the spice paste:
- 5 shallots (1/2 cup, 150g), peeled
- 4 cloves of garlic, peeled
- 2-4 red chilies, deseeded
- 2 tbsp of fresh ginger, grated or finely diced
- 1 tsp of ground turmeric
- 1 tsp of ground coriander/cilantro
- 1 tsp of ground cumin
- 1 tsp of ground cinnamon
- 1 tsp of ground fennel seeds
- 1 tsp of ground black pepper

For the Curry:
- 2 tbsp of canola (rapeseed) oil
- 4 tbsp of desiccated coconut
- 2 lbs (900g) of chicken thighs, deboned and deskinned, cut into 1-inch (2.5cm) cubes
- 1 can (400ml) of reduced fat coconut milk
- 2 cups (480ml) of water
- 2 stalks of lemongrass, bruised (bash with a rolling pin)
- 2 kaffir lime leaves
- 2 bay leaves
- 1 1/2 cups (250g) white rice, dry
- Salt and sugar, to taste
- Food processor or blender

INSTRUCTIONS

1. Assemble, measure, and prepare the ingredients.
2. In a blender or food processor, blend the spice paste ingredients until smooth (shallots, garlic, chilies, ginger, spices).
3. Next, add 2 tbsp of oil to a large pot or Dutch oven, heat on medium. Add the spice paste and cook for 5-7 minutes, until fragrant.
4. Meanwhile, add the desiccated coconut flakes to a dry frying pan over a gentle heat and toast until lightly browned (watch carefully as it can burn quickly).
5. Once the spice mix is fragrant, add the toasted coconut, chicken thighs, coconut milk, water, lemongrass, kaffir lime leaves, and bay leaves. Bring to a boil, then reduce heat to low and simmer for 1 1/2 - 2 hours (no lid) or until the meat is tender and the sauce thickens. Stir occasionally.
6. Twenty minutes before the curry is ready, cook the rice according to package instructions.
7. Once cooked, season the curry with salt and sugar to taste.
8. Serve the rendang curry over the rice.

VEGGIE THAI RED CURRY

EACH SERVING

| 770g | 580 | 7% | 30% | 63% |
| CARBON | CALORIES | PROTEIN | FAT | CARBS |

BALANCED MACRONUTRIENTS

Serves: 4   Prep Time: 10 mins   Cooking Time: 20 mins

THAI RED CURRY is called geng phet in Thai, which means 'spicy curry'. Red chilies provide the color and spicy flavor which are balanced by creamy coconut milk, tangy fish sauce, and the zing of fresh lime. Red curry is usually made with meat, but we think this dish works great with sweet potatoes, baby corn, and crunchy veggies.

CLIMATE KITCHEN HACKS this is a great dish to make veggie. The tangy red curry paste and creamy coconut flavors infuse into the veggies. The same serving size has an 35% lower carbon footprint, 20% fewer calories, and 45% less fat than chicken-based red curry recipes.

Classic Curries

INGREDIENTS

- 1 1/2 cups (250g) jasmine rice, dry
- 2 sweet potatoes (400g), peeled and cubed
- 8 sprays canola (rapeseed) oil
- 2-4 tbsp Thai red curry paste
- 1 can (400ml) coconut milk
- 1 cup (240ml) chicken or vegetable broth/stock
- 2 tbsp fish sauce
- 1 tbsp brown sugar
- 1 cup (240g) baby corn, halved
- 1 cup bok choy or baby bok choy (120g), leaves separated
- 1 yellow bell pepper (120g), sliced
- 1 red bell pepper (120g), sliced
- 1 zucchini/courgette (180g), sliced
- 1 onion (150g), finely diced
- 2 tbsp lime juice, freshly squeezed
- 1/4 cup fresh cilantro/coriander, chopped

INSTRUCTIONS

1. Assemble, measure, and prepare the ingredients. Use 2 tbsp red curry paste for a milder curry and 4 tbsp for heat.
2. Cook the rice according to package instructions and once ready reserve.
3. Meanwhile, place the sweet potato in a microwavable dish and heat on full for 6-8 mins until nearly cooked through (should be just going soft in the middle).
4. Next, spray oil into a large saucepan to coat, heat on a medium heat. Add the red curry paste to the saucepan and fry for 1-2 minutes until fragrant (add more oil if needed). Mix in the coconut milk, broth, fish sauce, and brown sugar. Stir to combine.
5. Add the microwaved sweet potato, baby corn, bok choi, red and yellow bell peppers, zucchini, and onion to the saucepan. Stir to coat the vegetables in the curry sauce. Bring the curry to a simmer and cook for 10-12 minutes, with a lid loosely covering the pan, until the veggies are cooked but still have a little bite.
6. Once the curry is cooked through, remove from the heat and stir in the lime juice to taste, and stir through half the cilantro/coriander.
7. Serve the curry over the cooked rice with the remaining cilantro/coriander on top.

BUNNY CHOW

EACH SERVING

470g	790	23%	23%	54%
CARBON	CALORIES	PROTEIN	FAT	CARBS

LOW IN SATURATED FAT

Serves: 4 | Prep Time: 10 mins | Cooking Time: 40 mins

BUNNY CHOW is a curry dish served up in a hollowed-out loaf of bread. The dish originated from the Indian community in Durban, South Africa during apartheid as a portable meal for the black and Indian community who were banned from sitting and eating in many restaurants. The dish is not made from rabbit but rather bunny comes from the term 'bania' which means merchant in Sanskrit.

CLIMATE KITCHEN HACKS we switch the traditional beef or lamb for chicken thighs, and we spray rather than drizzle the oil. The same serving size has a 90% lower carbon footprint and 10% less fat than traditional beef-based recipes.

Classic Curries

INGREDIENTS

- 1 large sweet potato (240g), peeled and diced
- 8 sprays of canola (rapeseed) oil
- 1 lb (450g) of chicken thighs, deboned and deskinned, cut into 1-inch (2.5cm) cubes
- 1 large onion (1 cup, 240g), finely chopped
- 1 tbsp of fresh ginger, grated
- 2 cloves of garlic, minced/crushed
- 2 tsp of ground cumin
- 2 tsp of ground coriander
- 1 tsp of ground turmeric
- 1/2 tsp ground fennel seeds
- 1/4 - 1 tsp of ground cayenne pepper
- 4 curry leaves
- Salt and pepper to taste
- 1 can (14.5 oz/411g) of diced tomatoes
- 1 red bell pepper (120g), sliced
- 2 cups (480ml) of water
- 4 cob loaves of bread / or 2 larger loaves, hollowed out (about 600g bread)
- 2-3 spring onions, sliced, to serve
- 1 carrot, grated, to serve

INSTRUCTIONS

1. Assemble, measure, and prepare the ingredients. Use 1/4 tsp cayenne pepper for warmth, 1/2 tsp for a kick, and 1 tsp or more for heat. You can always add more at the end.

2. Place the diced sweet potato into a microwaveable dish and microwave for 5 minutes (800W power) to part cook.

3. Meanwhile, spray oil into a skillet or heavy frying pan to coat and heat on high until smoking hot. Add the chicken and cook for 5-7 minutes until browned on all sides (spray more oil as required).

4. Next, spray oil in another large frying pan or saucepan and place over a medium-high heat. Add the onion and cook for 2-3 minutes until softened, add the ginger and cook for another 1-2 minutes, add the garlic, and cook for a further 30 seconds.

5. To the onion pan, add the cumin, coriander, turmeric, ground fennel seeds, cayenne pepper, curry leaves, and a pinch of salt & pepper. Cook for 1-2 minutes, until fragrant. Stir in the browned chicken, diced tomatoes, sliced bell pepper, part-cooked sweet potato, and water. Bring to a simmer.

6. Reduce the heat to low, cover loosely (to allow the steam to escape) and simmer for 30 minutes, until the meat is cooked through, and the sauce thickened (take the lid off completely for the last 10 minutes if it needs to thicken further).

7. Hollow out the bread loaves, leaving a thick bread "bowl" to hold the curry. Fill the bread bowls with curry and serve with a sprinkling of spring onion/carrot on top.

SHIITAKE CHOW MEIN

EACH SERVING

470g	640	9%	23%	68%
CARBON	CALORIES	PROTEIN	FAT	CARBS

BALANCED MACRONUTRIENTS • LOW IN SATURATED FAT
VEGAN OPTION

Serves: 4   Prep Time: 10 mins   Cooking Time: 20 mins

CHOW MEIN is a traditional Chinese dish of thin noodles and crunchy veggies in a flavorful sauce. When the dish was first popularized in America in the 1850s it became more meat heavy, and with egg fried noodles and a thicker sauce. Our vegan recipe returns chow mein to its veggie roots - the perfect combination of meaty shiitake & chestnut mushrooms combined with crunchy carrots, tender broccoli, and toasted cashew nuts gives this chow mein great texture and unrivalled taste.

CLIMATE KITCHEN HACKS we switch the meat for mushrooms in our delicious chow mein recipe. The same serving size has a 90% lower carbon footprint, 10% fewer calories, and 30% less fat than beef-based chow mein recipes.

INGREDIENTS

- 4 servings of wheat noodles (2/3 lb, 300g, dry weight, vegan option)
- 8 sprays of canola (rapeseed) oil
- 1 large onion (1 cup, 240g), thick sliced
- 2 tbsp fresh ginger, grated or finely diced
- 4 cloves of garlic, minced/crushed
- 2 cups (240g) tenderstem/baby broccoli
- 2-3 carrots (1 cup, 240g), peeled halved and sliced lengthways
- 1 1/2 cups (180g) shiitake mushrooms, sliced
- 1 1/2 cups (180g) chestnut or Portobello mushrooms, sliced
- 1/4 cup (60g) cashews, roughly chopped (fairtrade certified)
- 2 tbsp sesame seeds
- 6 tbsp (90ml) of soy sauce
- 1 1/2 tbsp of sesame oil
- 4 green/spring onions (1/4 cup, 60g), sliced

INSTRUCTIONS

1. Assemble, measure, and prepare the ingredients.
2. Cook the noodles according to the package instructions and set aside once cooked.
3. Meanwhile, spray 4 sprays of oil in a wok or large frying pan to coat, and heat on medium-high. Add the onion and fry for 2-3 minutes until softened, add the ginger and fry for another 1-2 minutes until fragrant, add the garlic and fry for another 30 seconds. Add the broccoli, carrots, and two types of mushrooms, spray with the remaining 4 sprays of oil, and stir-fry for an additional 4-6 minutes until the vegetables are tender and cooked through (retaining a little bite).
4. While the vegetables cook, take a small pan (no oil), add the cashews and sesame seeds and heat gently until lightly toasted/browned (watch careful to avoid burning). Set aside.
5. Next, add the cooked noodles, soy sauce, and sesame oil to the vegetables and toss everything together until the noodles and vegetables are evenly coated in the sauce.
6. Serve hot, garnished with sliced green/spring onions, plus the toasted cashews & sesame seeds.

KUNG PAO CHICKEN

EACH SERVING

660g	690	22%	30%	48%
CARBON	CALORIES	PROTEIN	FAT	CARBS

Serves: 4   Prep Time: 10 mins   Cooking Time: 15 mins

KUNG PAO is a translation of the Chinese word Gōngbǎo which means palace guardian. The dish was invented by Ding Baozhen who was Gōngbǎo and protector of the prince during the Qing Dynasty in the late 19th Century. Kung Pao is now a worldwide phenomenon, and this recipe won't disappoint; made with stir-fried chicken, crunchy peanuts, and tender vegetables in a tangy, spiced sauce.

CLIMATE KITCHEN HACKS go easy on the oil and this dish is already low carbon with a good nutritional balance.

Fake-aways

INGREDIENTS

- 1 1/2 cups (250g) rice, dry
- 1 lb (450g) of boneless, skinless chicken breast, cut into small cubes
- 1/4 cup (40g) of cornstarch
- 12 sprays of canola (rapeseed) oil
- 1 large onion (240g), thick sliced
- 2 cloves of garlic, minced/crushed
- 2 carrots (1 cup, 150g), peeled, halved and sliced
- 2 bell peppers (2 cup, 240g), sliced
- 1/2 cup (60g) of peanuts
- 2 tbsp of soy sauce
- 2 tbsp of rice vinegar
- 2 tbsp of hoisin sauce
- 1-2 tsp of ground Szechuan peppercorn (or black pepper)
- 1 tsp of sugar
- 4 green/spring onions (1/4 cup, 50g), thinly sliced

INSTRUCTIONS

1. Assemble, measure, and prepare the ingredients.
2. Cook the rice according to package instructions and set aside once done.
3. While the rice is cooking, toss the chicken cubes in the cornstarch to coat. Place the coated chicken in a sieve or colander and shake to remove excess flour (stops the chicken becoming too gloopy).
4. Spray 4 sprays of oil into a skillet or heavy frying pan to coat and heat on high until smoking hot. Add the chicken pieces and fry for 7-8 minutes, adding more oil as required to keep it sizzling. Cook until the chicken is browned on all sides and cooked through (you can test by cutting the largest piece in half and checking there is no pink). Set Aside.
5. Next, take a large wok, spray with a few sprays of oil to coat, and heat on medium-high. Add the onion and stir-fry for 2-3 minutes, add the garlic and cook for another 30 seconds, then finally add the cooked chicken, carrots, peppers, peanuts, soy sauce, rice vinegar, hoisin sauce, Szechuan peppercorn and sugar. Stir-fry for 2-3 minutes.
6. Serve hot, garnished with sliced green/spring onions and a side of rice.

LEAN SWEET & SOUR CHICKEN

EACH SERVING

800g	680	23%	21%	56%
CARBON	CALORIES	PROTEIN	FAT	CARBS

LOW IN SATURATED FAT

Serves: 4   Prep Time: 10 mins   Cooking Time: 15 mins

SWEET AND SOUR is a classic Chinese dish made with deep-fried pork and a tangy sweet and sour sauce. The traditional recipe is usually deep fried which means lots of high carbon footprint oil and saturated fat. Our recipe uses lightly battered chicken and just a couple of tablespoons of oil, meaning it's much better for you and for the planet.

CLIMATE KITCHEN HACKS we use chicken fillet, which is a higher carbon cut, but we switch some meat with extra vegetables to add greater depth of flavor, texture and to save on carbon footprint. We go easy on the batter and lightly fry in minimal oil. The same serving size has a 40% lower carbon footprint, 10% fewer calories, and 40% less saturated fat compared to deep fried sweet and sour pork.

Fake-aways

INGREDIENTS

- 1/2 lb (225g) white/brown/wholegrain rice
- 1/8 cup (15g) of cornstarch
- 1/4 cup (30g) of all-purpose flour
- 1 egg
- 1/4 cup (60ml) of water
- 1 lb (450g) of chicken fillet/breast, cut into bite-size pieces
- 1/4 cup (60g) of ketchup
- 2 tbsp of rice vinegar
- 2 tbsp of soy sauce
- 1 tbsp of brown sugar
- 1 tsp of cornstarch
- 1/4 tsp of white pepper
- 2 tbsp plus 16 sprays of canola (rapeseed) oil
- 1 small onion (1/2 cup, 120g), peeled, halved and thick sliced
- 2 bell peppers (2 cup, 240g), red and green cubed
- 2 carrots (1 cup, 150g), peeled halved and thin sliced
- 1 cup (200g) baby corn, halved lengthways
- 1/2 cup (120g) of canned pineapple, diced
- 3-4 green/spring onion, sliced

INSTRUCTIONS

1. Assemble, measure, and prepare the ingredients.
2. Cook the rice according to the package instructions and set aside.
3. Meanwhile, toss the chicken cubes in cornstarch to coat.
4. In a medium bowl, mix the flour, egg and water until a thick, smooth batter is formed. Add the chicken cubes to the mixture, coat well, then transfer into a sieve or colander and mix around to remove excess coating.
5. In a small bowl, mix the ketchup, rice vinegar, soy sauce, brown sugar, cornstarch and white pepper.
6. Next, heat 2 tbsp of the oil in a heavy skillet pan over a high heat until the oil is smoking hot. Carefully add the coated chicken to the hot oil and fry for about 7-8 minutes until golden brown. Spray with extra oil during cooking if necessary to keep it sizzling. Remove the pan from the heat and set aside. Check the chicken is cooked through by cutting the largest piece in half to check it is white through (no pink in the middle).
7. Finally, place a wok or frying pan over a medium-high heat with a few sprays of oil. Fry the onion for 2-3 minutes until softened then add the bell pepper, carrots, baby corn, and pineapple. Heat for 1 minute whilst tossing. Add the sauce mix and stir through.
8. Add the fried chicken, toss to coat with the sauce, heat through for 2-3 minutes. Serve hot over the rice with sliced green/spring onion sprinkled on top.

SCALLOP PAD THAI

EACH SERVING

310g	460	14%	27%	59%
CARBON	CALORIES	PROTEIN	FAT	CARBS

LOW IN SATURATED FAT • BALANCED MACRONUTRIENTS
LOW CALORIE

Serves: 4   Prep Time: 20 mins   Cooking Time: 15 mins

PAD THAI is the national dish of Thailand, picked by Prime Minister Phibun after taking power at the end of World War II when he renamed the country Thailand (formerly Siam) and ran a competition to create a new national dish. Pad Thai won and it's still winning today! Our recipe uses fluffy rice noodles, delicate scallops, and vibrant veggies balanced by a tangy fresh sauce.

CLIMATE KITCHEN HACKS we switch crustaceans for mollusks – by using scallops instead of shrimp it makes Pad Thai super low carbon and even more delicious. Just make sure the scallops are sustainably farmed or hand caught. The same serving size has a 70% lower carbon footprint compared to shrimp/prawn Pad Thai recipes.

Fake-aways

INGREDIENTS

- 4 portions of rice noodles (180g / 5oz)
- 12 sprays of canola (rapeseed) oil
- 1 large onion (1 1/2 cup, 240g), thick sliced
- 2 cloves of garlic, minced/crushed
- 3/4 cup (180g) of fresh or frozen scallops (sustainably farmed not dredged at sea), defrosted
- 1 cup (120g) of red bell pepper, sliced
- 2 carrots (1 cup, 150g), peeled halved and thin sliced
- 2 cups (240g) tenderstem/baby broccoli
- 3 tbsp of soy sauce
- 3 tbsp of fish sauce
- 3 tbsp of brown sugar
- 1 1/2 tbsp of tamarind paste
- 1 1/2 tbsp of lime juice, freshly squeezed
- 4 green/spring onions (1/4 cup, 60g), thinly sliced
- 1/4 cup (60g) of dry roasted peanuts, roughly chopped
- Lime wedges, to serve

INSTRUCTIONS

1. Assemble, measure, and prepare the ingredients.
2. Soak the rice noodles in warm water for two thirds of the time given on the packet instructions so they are not fully cooked/soft. Drain in cold water, spray with 1 spray of oil to stop the noodles sticking together and set aside.
3. Meanwhile, heat 4 sprays of the oil in a wok or large skillet over a medium-high heat. Add the onion and cook until softened (2-3 mins), add the garlic and fry for another 30 seconds. Set aside on a separate plate.
4. Spray another 4 sprays of the oil in the now empty wok/skillet, turn the heat up to high, wait until the oil is smoking hot and add the scallops. Fry for 1 minute on each side of the scallops (turn once using tongs) so the tops turn golden brown. Set aside on the plate with the onions and garlic.
5. Spray another 4 sprays of oil in the now empty wok/skillet, turn the heat up to high, and add the vegetables (bell peppers, carrots, and broccoli) to the smoking hot oil. Stir-fry for 3-4 minutes until the vegetables are tender but still have some crunch.
6. Stir in the cooked onions, cooked scallops, soy sauce, fish sauce, brown sugar, and tamarind paste, mix well, and remove from the heat. Add the lime juice to the rice noodles to loosen the strands and add the noodles/lime to the main wok/skillet.
7. Toss everything together until the noodles, scallops, and vegetables are evenly coated in the sauce.
8. Serve hot, garnished with sliced green onions, chopped peanuts, and lime wedges.

CHICKEN GYROS

EACH SERVING

400g	670	32%	36%	32%
CARBON	CALORIES	PROTEIN	FAT	CARBS

HIGH PROTEIN

- Serves: 4
- Marinate Time: 120 mins
- Prep Time: 10 mins
- Cooking Time: 20 mins

GYROS is a popular Greek dish made with meat cooked on a vertical rotisserie, similar to the Turkish Döner Kebab. Our recipe can be made at home and tastes just as good - with succulent chicken, tangy tomatoes, and crispy chips wrapped up in a doughy flat bread blanket.

CLIMATE KITCHEN HACKS we switch the lamb for chicken thighs. We use natural yogurt rather than Greek yogurt (it uses 4x less milk to make) and we go easy on the oil. The same serving size has a 90% lower carbon footprint, 5% fewer calories, and 15% less fat compared to lamb gyros recipes.

Fake-aways

INGREDIENTS

- 1 1/2 tsp of dried oregano
- 1 1/2 tsp of garlic powder
- 3 tsp paprika powder
- 1/2 tsp of salt
- 1/2 tsp of black pepper
- 1 1/2 lb (680g) chicken thighs, deboned & skinned
- 2-3 large potatoes (480g), cut into fries (no need to peel)
- 8 sprays of canola (rapeseed) oil
- 4-6 flatbreads
- 2 tomatoes (1 cup, 240g), sliced
- 1/2 red onion (1/2 cup, 120g), thinly sliced
- 2 tbsp pickled red onion slices, to serve
- 2 cups (120g) of shredded lettuce (Romano or iceberg work well)
- 1/2 cup (120ml) garlic sauce or tzatziki

INSTRUCTIONS

1. Mix the oregano, garlic powder, 2 tsp of paprika, salt and pepper in a bowl. Rub the mixture over the chicken thighs and marinate for at least 2 hours in the refrigerator.
2. Once the chicken is marinated, preheat a fan oven to 425ºF / 220ºC / Gas mark 7 (for a non-fan oven 465ºF / 240ºC / Gas mark 8).
3. Cut the potatoes into fries and place in a bowl of cold salty water to draw the moisture from the potato and help the fries crisp up.
4. Assemble, measure, and prepare the other ingredients.
5. Drain the fries and pat dry with a tea-towel or soft kitchen paper. Spread the dry fries evenly over a large baking tray (make sure they have plenty of space on the tray to ensure they go crispy), spray with 4 sprays of the oil to coat, sprinkle over 1 tsp paprika, salt and pepper. Place in the pre-heated oven for 25 minutes until cooked through and crisp.
6. Whilst the fries cook, take the marinated chicken out of the refrigerator, and place the whole thighs on a wire rack and the wire rack on a baking tray. Carefully place in the hot oven with the fries and cook for 20 minutes until the chicken is browned and cooked through (no pink when cut open through the middle).
7. Warm the pita bread / flatbread in the oven a few minutes before serving up. To assemble the gyros, slice the warm chicken and arrange on the flatbread, top with sliced tomato, onion, lettuce, the cooked fries and garlic or tzatziki sauce.
8. You can leave the Gyros open or roll them up. If you wrap some brown paper around the bottom half of the flatbread this will help to hold the rolls together.

YAKISOBA CHICKEN

EACH SERVING

610g	560	27%	27%	46%
CARBON	CALORIES	PROTEIN	FAT	CARBS

Serves: 4　　　Prep Time: 10 mins　　　Cooking Time: 15 mins

YAKISOBA is a popular Japanese dish made with stir-fried wheat noodles and cabbage. It became popular in Japan after World War II when wheat became expensive, so chow mein type dishes were bulked out with cabbage. Our recipe is quick, easy, and tastes great with vibrant pickled ginger balanced by sweet chicken and crunchy, fresh veggies.

CLIMATE KITCHEN HACKS chicken yakisoba is a naturally low carbon dish.

Fake-aways

INGREDIENTS

- 12 oz (250g, dry weight) of Chinese-style wheat/egg noodles
- 9 sprays canola (rapeseed) oil
- 1 small onion (1/2 cup, 120g), thick sliced
- 2 cloves of garlic, minced/crushed
- 2 cups (460g) of chicken breast, thick sliced
- 1/2 small green/savoy cabbage (2 cups, 240g), thick sliced
- 3 bell peppers (450g, 3 cups), red, yellow and green, sliced
- 2 tbsp of soy sauce
- 2 tbsp of Worcestershire sauce
- 2 tbsp of oyster sauce
- 1 tbsp of sugar
- 2 tsp of sesame oil
- 4 green/spring onions (1/4 cup, 60g), thinly sliced
- 1/4 cup (60g) of beni shoga / pickled ginger

INSTRUCTIONS

1. Assemble, measure, and prepare the ingredients.
2. Cook the noodles according to the package instructions and set aside.
3. Heat 3 sprays of the oil in a wok or large skillet over a medium-high heat. Add the onion and cook until softened (2-3 mins), then add the garlic and fry for another 30 seconds. Set aside on a separate plate.
4. Return the wok to a high heat, spray another 3 sprays of oil, once the oil is smoking hot add the sliced chicken and stir-fry for 6-8 minutes until the chicken is browned on all sides and cooked through (if you are unsure check by cutting through the largest piece to check it is not pink in the middle). Set aside on a separate plate.
5. Return the wok to a high heat, spray the final 3 sprays of oil, and once the oil is smoking hot add the cabbage and bell peppers and stir-fry for 3-4 minutes until the vegetables go tender but still crunchy.
6. Stir in the cooked onions, cooked chicken, cooked noodles, soy sauce, Worcestershire sauce, oyster sauce, sugar, and sesame oil. Toss everything together until the noodles and vegetables are evenly coated in the sauce.
7. Serve hot, garnished with sliced green onions and beni shoga (pickled ginger).

EASY SCALLOP RISOTTO

EACH SERVING

460g	580	13%	26%	61%
CARBON	CALORIES	PROTEIN	FAT	CARBS

BALANCED MACRONUTRIENTS

Serves: 4   Prep Time: 10 mins   Cooking Time: 25 mins

RISOTTO is a classic Italian rice dish cooked with broth and starchy rice to create a creamy consistency. Many home-cooks are hesitant to cook risotto as recipes are often labor-intensive, requiring that you ladle one spoonful of broth at a time whilst stirring continuously. Well, we have perfected the low-stir, easy risotto. The secret is to toast a portion of the Arborio rice on the bottom of the pan to create a delicious nutty flavor. But to leave another portion of the rice untoasted so that the starch inside remains intact and can create the creamy texture. We combine the creamy, nutty rice with rich parmesan cheese, luscious scallops, and fresh mint.

CLIMATE KITCHEN HACKS scallop risotto is a low carbon twist on traditional white fish risottos. Replace the emissions intensive white fish with scallops, peas, and mint for a fresh take on an Italian classic. The same serving size has a 60% lower carbon footprint than traditional fish risotto.

Soul Bowls

INGREDIENTS

- 2 tbsp olive oil
- 1 onion (1 cup, 150g), finely diced
- 2 cloves garlic, minced/crushed
- 1 1/2 cups (300g) Arborio rice (dry, don't rinse)
- 1/2 cup (120ml) white wine
- 3 cups (720ml) fish or chicken stock
- 1/2 lb (225g) small scallops (sustainably farmed)
- 2 tbsp (30g) butter
- 2 cups (240g) frozen peas
- 1/4 cup (25g) grated Parmesan cheese
- 2-3 leaves of fresh mint, chopped (no more or it will overpower the dish)
- Salt and pepper, to taste
- Lemon Wedges, to serve

INSTRUCTIONS

1. Assemble, measure, and prepare the ingredients.
2. In a large saucepan or Dutch oven, heat the 2 tbsp of olive oil over a medium heat. Add the onion and cook until softened (2-3 mins), add the garlic and fry for another 30 seconds.
3. Stir in the rice and then let the rice cook for about 1 minute without any further stirring. This allows the rice on the bottom of the pan to toast, adding a nutty flavor to the risotto, but the rice on top still retains starch to help create the creamy texture of the dish.
4. Pour in the white wine and stir until absorbed. Next add the fish or chicken stock, stir through, bring to a simmer, turn the heat to low, loosely cover (so that some steam can escape) and leave to cook for 20-25 minutes, stirring occasionally.
5. Whilst the rice cooks, take a heavy frying pan or skillet, add 3-4 sprays of oil and heat on high until the oil is smoking hot. Add the scallops to the pan and fry on the first side for 30 seconds, flip the scallops, fry for 30 seconds on the other side, then remove the pan from the heat and add 2 tbsp of butter and move the pan to allow the butter to coat the browned scallops.
6. Once the stock has been absorbed by the rice, taste it and ensure the rice has softened but still has some bite. Add the browned scallops and peas and continue to cook for an additional 2-5 minutes until the rice is cooked to your preference (it should retain a little bite) and the scallops are cooked through.
7. Remove from the heat and stir in the grated Parmesan cheese and fresh mint. Season with salt and pepper to taste.
8. Serve immediately with a lemon wedge.

SIMPLE SEAFOOD PAELLA

EACH SERVING

510g	660	26%	28%	46%
CARBON	CALORIES	PROTEIN	FAT	CARBS

Serves: 4   Prep Time: 10 mins   Cooking Time: 35 mins

PAELLA originates from Valencia, Spain, where the word 'paella' means frying pan. Our paella recipe combines rich, creamy rice with salty mussels, sweet chorizo, and succulent chicken. It's a perfect dish for sharing with friends and family.

CLIMATE KITCHEN HACKS we switch the crustaceans for mollusks; instead of using shrimp or crayfish we use clams and/or mussels. This is because shrimp have a high carbon footprint owing to the destruction of wetlands through aquaculture or destruction of the seabed by trawling at sea. Mollusks can be sustainably farmed on coastal areas where they filter the water and improve the aquatic environment. The same serving size has a 70% lower carbon footprint than shrimp-based recipes.

Soul Bowls

INGREDIENTS

- 8 sprays canola (rapeseed) oil
- 1/2 lb (225g) chicken breast, cut into bite-sized pieces
- 1/4 lb (110g) chorizo sausage, diced
- 1 large onion (1 cup, 150g), diced
- 2 red bell peppers (2 cup, 240g), diced
- 2 cloves garlic, minced/crushed
- 1 1/2 cups (300g) bomba or arborio rice, dry (do not rinse)
- 3 cups (720ml) chicken or vegetable broth/stock
- 1/2 tsp saffron threads (optional)
- 1 lb (450g) of shell-on clams or mussels, cleaned and scrubbed (sustainably farmed - fresh, frozen or vac-packed)
- 1 cup (120g) frozen peas
- Salt and pepper, to taste
- Lemon wedges, for serving (optional)

INSTRUCTIONS

1. Assemble, measure, and prepare the ingredients. Saffron is optional as it is expensive and can be difficult to source - it adds a floral/aromatic flavor to the dish which some love and others don't!

2. In a heavy frying pan or skillet spray 4 sprays of oil and heat on high until smoking hot. Add the chicken breast pieces and fry for 4-5 minutes until lightly browned. Add the chorizo and cook for another 2-3 minutes to crisp up the chorizo and release the oils and flavors.

3. Next in a large paella pan or wide skillet, heat 4 sprays of oil over a medium-high heat. Add the onion and fry for 2-3 minutes to soften, add the bell pepper for a further 1-2 minutes, then the garlic for the final 30 seconds.

4. Add the browned chicken and chorizo to the onion and pepper pan. Mix well, then add the dry rice and let it cook for about 1 minute without stirring so the rice becomes lightly toasted on the bottom (this adds a nutty flavor whilst the rice on the top retains its starch content to create a creaminess).

5. Next, pour the broth into the chorizo pan to capture all that flavorful chorizo oil (deglaze) and then pour the broth into the rice pan, add the saffron (if using), and bring the mixture to a simmer.

6. Reduce the heat to low, cover the pan, and cook for about 18-20 minutes until the rice is tender (but still has a little bite) and the liquid has been fully absorbed.

7. Meanwhile, as the rice simmers, cook the clams or mussels according to packet instructions. If using fresh clams or mussels, first clean them in salted cold water. Then boil a pan of water and add the cleaned mussels and/or clams, place the lid on firmly to make sure they steam for 5-10 minutes until they have all opened (discard any unopened clams or mussels as they are not good to eat).

8. Once the rice is cooked through, stir in the peas and cooked clams and/or mussels and simmer for an additional 2 minutes. Taste, and adjust the salt and pepper as needed.

9. Serve the paella with lemon wedges on the side.

SMOKY MACKEREL KEDGEREE

EACH SERVING

420g	620	25%	25%	50%
CARBON	CALORIES	PROTEIN	FAT	CARBS

Serves: 4   Prep Time: 10 mins   Cooking Time: 45 mins

KEDGEREE is a fishy rice dish originally invented in the coastal villages of India where it is traditionally served at breakfast. The dish became very popular with Scottish soldiers stationed in India who brought it back to the UK and started using smoked haddock as their fish of choice. Our version of the recipe uses smoked mackerel fillets, creamy egg, and a gentle blend of spices to create a warm, comforting bowl of goodness that can be enjoyed any time of the day.

CLIMATE KITCHEN HACKS we use smoked mackerel rather than the more traditional haddock. Mackerel is more abundant than haddock and swims in the ocean mid-waters in large schools meaning the fish are easier to catch, the boats use less fuel, and therefore mackerel has a low carbon footprint. The same serving size has a 70% lower carbon footprint than recipes using smoked white fish like haddock.

Soul Bowls

INGREDIENTS

- 1 lb (450g) smoked mackerel fillets, deboned and skin removed (it should peel off easily)
- 2 cups (480ml) water
- 1 bay leaf
- 1 large onion (1 cup, 240g), peeled and quartered
- 2 cups (350g) basmati rice
- 1/2 tsp turmeric powder
- 1/4 tsp cayenne pepper
- Salt and pepper, to taste
- 4 medium/large eggs, at room tempe
- 1/2 cup (60g) frozen peas
- 2 tbsp butter
- 2 tbsp chopped fresh parsley
- 4 tbsp crème fraiche, to serve

INSTRUCTIONS

1. Assemble, measure, and prepare the ingredients.
2. Place the smoked mackerel in a large saucepan with 2 cups of water, the bay leaf and onion. Bring to a boil and then reduce the heat to low. Cover and simmer for about 8-10 minutes until the fish is warmed through.
3. Remove the fish from the pan and reserve the cooking liquid. Flake the fish with a fork and set aside.
4. Rinse the rice in cold water (using a sieve and bowl) until the water runs clear. Drain the rice and add it to the pan with the reserved cooking liquid. Add turmeric powder, cayenne pepper, and a good pinch of salt & pepper. Bring to a boil, then reduce the heat to low, cover and simmer to cook the rice according to packet instructions (usually 18-20 mins), you may need to add a little more water towards the end if it looks dry.
5. Whilst the kedgeree rice is cooking through, boil a pan of water, prick the blunt end of the eggs to allow the air to escape (this stops them cracking and leaking), boil the eggs for 7 minutes to set the white and leave the yolk sticky. Remove from the pan and place in cold water to cool and stop cooking, then peel. Cut two eggs into quarters and two eggs into halves.
6. Once the rice is cooked through, remove the kedgeree rice pan from the heat, add the peas, flaked fish, and butter. Mix the ingredients through the rice and let the rice mixture sit for 5 minutes before fluffing with a fork.
7. Stir in the parsley and 2 tbsp of crème fraiche then gently mix through the quartered hard-boiled eggs. Season with salt and pepper to taste.
8. Serve the kedgeree hot or warm, garnished with the hard-boiled egg halves on top, 1/2 tbsp crème fraiche per serving and extra parsley if desired.

CHICKEN BIRYANI

EACH SERVING

340g	560	26%	31%	43%
CARBON	CALORIES	PROTEIN	FAT	CARBS

Serves: 4   Prep Time: 10 mins   Cooking Time: 50 mins

BIRYANI is a traditional dish from the Indian subcontinent. An aromatic rice dish that is usually made with meat or vegetables and a variety of spices. It is typically cooked in a sealed pot which allows the flavors to infuse.

CLIMATE KITCHEN HACKS we make sure to use the traditional chicken leg or thigh cuts, rather than chicken breast, which means a 40% lower carbon footprint and a more flavorful dish. Cut back on oil and you can reduce the fat content by 20%.

Soul Bowls

INGREDIENTS

- 12 sprays of canola (rapeseed) oil
- 1 large onion (1 cup, 240g), finely diced
- 1 1/2 tbsp ginger paste
- 2 cloves garlic, minced/crushed
- 1 lb (450g) boneless chicken thighs, cut into bite-sized pieces
- 1 1/2 tsp turmeric powder
- 1 1/2 tsp cumin powder
- 1 1/2 tsp coriander/cilantro powder
- 1/2 - 1 tsp red chili powder
- 1 tsp garam masala powder
- 1 cup (240ml) water
- 1 1/2 cups (250g) basmati rice
- 2 cups (480ml) chicken stock/broth
- 4 tbsp sultanas (optional)
- 4 tbsp yogurt (plain, soy, or oat)
- 4 tbsp cilantro/coriander, chopped,
- Salt and pepper, to taste
- 4 tbsp flaked almonds, to serve

INSTRUCTIONS

1. Assemble, measure, and prepare the ingredients. Use 1/2 tsp red chili for a mild spice flavor, 1 tsp for some heat, and more if you like it hot!
2. In a large pot or Dutch oven, heat 4 sprays of the oil over medium-high heat. Add the onion and fry for 3-4 minutes until softened, add the ginger paste and garlic and fry for another 30 seconds until fragrant, and the onions lightly browned.
3. Spray with another 4 sprays of oil, add the chicken pieces, and stir through. Next add the turmeric, cumin, coriander/cilantro powder, red chili powder, and garam masala. Spray with the final 4 sprays of the oil and cook for 2-3 minutes until the chicken is seared on the outside (but not cooked through) and the spices fragrant.
4. Pour in the 1 cup of water, bring to a boil, then reduce the heat to low. Cover and simmer for 15 minutes until the chicken is cooked through.
5. While the chicken is cooking, rinse the rice in several changes of water until the water runs clear (use a sieve and bowl). Drain the rice and add it to the pot with chicken. Add the 2 cups of stock/broth and bring it to a boil.
6. Reduce the heat to low, cover the pot and simmer for 18-20 minutes or until the rice is cooked and water is absorbed.
7. Remove the pot from the heat, fluff the rice with a fork, add the sultanas, half the yogurt, and half the cilantro/coriander, and mix through. Taste, and season with salt and pepper.
8. Serve the biryani with the flaked almonds plus the remaining cilantro and natural yogurt on top.

CRISPY PORK RAMEN BOWL

EACH SERVING

720g	660	32%	36%	32%
CARBON	CALORIES	PROTEIN	FAT	CARBS

Serves: 4   Prep Time: 10 mins   Cooking Time: 15 mins

RAMEN is a delicious noodle-based broth packed full of flavor. The first Ramen shop opened in Tokyo in 1910 serving soy sauce ramen. There are now dozens of regional variations made with different noodles, broth flavoring, and meats. Our version combines a miso and soy based broth with crispy pork belly slices, soft udon noodles, rich egg and a fresh zing of spring onion and ginger.

CLIMATE KITCHEN HACKS we use pork belly rather than beef. The same serving size has an 85% lower carbon footprint than traditional beef ramen recipes.

Soul Bowls

INGREDIENTS

- 1 lb (450g) pork belly strips
- 4 medium/large eggs, at room temperature
- 4 cups (1 litre) chicken stock/broth
- 4 tbsp (60ml) light soy sauce
- 4 tbsp (60ml) sake or rice wine
- 1 tbsp miso paste
- 2 cloves of garlic, minced/crushed
- 1 inch (2.5cm) ginger, grated or finely diced
- 4 servings of udon or ramen (soba) noodles (600g fresh, or 225g if using dried noodles)
- 4 green/spring onions (1/4 cup, 60g), sliced
- Sesame seeds to garnish

INSTRUCTIONS

1. Assemble, measure, and prepare the ingredients.
2. Heat a skillet or heavy frying pan over a high heat (no need for oil as the fat from the pork will suffice) and carefully place the pork slices onto the hot pan. Cook for 4-6 minutes on each side until nicely browned and crispy. Set aside to cool.
3. As the pork is cooking, boil a pan of water, prick the blunt end of the eggs to allow the air to escape (avoids cracking during cooking), boil the eggs for 7 minutes to set the white and leave the yolk sticky. Remove from the pan and place in cold water to cool and stop cooking.
4. Meanwhile, in a separate pot, bring the broth/stock, soy sauce, sake/rice wine, miso paste, garlic, and ginger to a simmer. Cook for 5 minutes to allow the flavors to combine.
5. Bring a pot of water to a boil and cook the ramen noodles according to the package instructions. Once cooked, rinse in cold water to remove excess starch and prevent overcooking, drain and set aside. Note: If you prefer to eat your Ramen with just a spoon you may wish to chop the noodles into smaller lengths at this point.
6. As the noodles are cooking through, peel and halve the boiled eggs, thinly slice the cooked pork and place on some kitchen paper to remove the excess fat. Divide the noodles between 4 bowls.
7. Taste the broth, add more soy sauce to taste. Then ladle the broth into the noodle bowls and top each bowl with the cooked pork, green onions, and boiled egg.
8. Garnish with sesame seeds and serve hot with some chopsticks and a spoon.

BIBIMBAP

EACH SERVING

680g	700	28%	40%	32%
CARBON	CALORIES	PROTEIN	FAT	CARBS

Serves: 4   Prep Time: 10 mins   Cooking Time: 15 mins

BIBIMBAP is a Korean dish of rice topped with delicious vegetables, chili sauce, and protein. The dish was popularized across the world in the late 1990s when Korean Air started serving it on the inflight menu. Our version will send your taste buds flying with crispy pork belly, spicy rice, and sumptuous fried egg.

CLIMATE KITCHEN HACKS we switch the traditional beef for pork belly. The same serving size has a 90% lower carbon footprint than traditional beef bibimbap recipes.

Soul Bowls

INGREDIENTS

- 1 1/2 cups (250g) dry short-grain (sushi) white rice
- 1 lb (450g) pork belly strips
- 1 small onion (1/2 cup, 120g), sliced
- 1 small carrot (1/2 cup, 120g), shredded/julienned
- 1 small zucchini/courgette (1/2 cup, 120g), shredded/julienned
- 2 cloves of garlic, minced/crushed
- 1/2 cup (120g) bean sprouts (optional if you can grab a small bag)
- Salt and pepper to taste
- 4 medium/large eggs
- 4 tbsp (60ml) gochujang Korean chili pepper paste (Siracha hot chili sauce also works well)
- 2 tbsp sesame oil
- 4 tbsp sesame seeds
- 4 green/spring onions (1/4 cup, 60g), thinly sliced

INSTRUCTIONS

1. Assemble, measure, and prepare the ingredients.
2. Preheat the oven to 175°F / 80°C / Gas mark 1 (for a non-fan oven 210°F / 100°C / Gas mark 1).
3. Cook the rice according to package instructions. Set aside and keep warm once cooked.
4. Heat a skillet or heavy frying pan over a high heat (no need for oil as the fat from the pork will suffice) and carefully place the pork strips onto the hot pan. Cook for 4-6 minutes on each side until nicely browned and crispy. Transfer the cooked pork to a plate, cover with foil, and leave in the oven to keep warm. Drain the excess fat from the pan but retain some for the next step.
5. In the same pan, on a medium heat, gently fry the onion for 2-3 minutes, then add the carrot and zucchini/courgette. Fry for another 1 minute. Add the garlic and bean sprouts (optional), and fry for a further 1 minute. Season with salt and pepper and transfer the vegetables to a plate in the warm oven.
6. In the same pan, fry the eggs to your liking.
7. To assemble the bibimbap. First slice the pork strips. Divide the rice among four bowls. Then arrange the pork, vegetables, and fried egg on top of the rice. Drizzle each bowl with 1 tbsp of gochujang (chili sauce) and 1/2 tbsp of sesame oil. Sprinkle 1 tbsp of sesame seeds and green onions over the top of each bowl.
8. Mix everything together into a delicious mess before eating.

THE SCIENCE BIT

We calculate the environmental and nutritional information for each of the recipes using science-based factors which provide carbon dioxide equivalent emissions, calories, and macro-nutrient content per unit weight of each of the ingredients used.

We repeat the calculations for both the standard original recipe and our modified (hacked) recipe based on the same serving weight. This allows for comparison of the carbon footprint, calories, and macronutrients per meal.

CARBON FOOTPRINT:

The carbon footprint is calculated using carbon dioxide equivalent emissions factors for carbon dioxide, methane, nitrous oxide, and fluorocarbons using 100-year global warming potentials. These factors provide the average greenhouse gas emissions released throughout the lifecycle of the food product from field to fork, this includes (but is not limited to) the following:

- » **Agriculture:** The direct and indirect emissions from land-use change, enteric fermentation, fertilizer run-off, and rice paddy dry down.

- » **Processing:** The emissions from energy used during the processing of raw food products.

- » **Packaging:** The emissions from producing metal, plastic, or cardboard packaging.

- » **Transport:** The emissions from fuel used in transporting and refrigerating food products.

The emissions factors are based on foods sourced globally and consumed in Europe with the food categorization and data based on FAOSTAT and EXIOBASE data subsets. Whilst the data is European centric, the calculations remain relevant in any area of the world because location-based emissions (such as transportation and refrigeration) form a relatively small part of the overall carbon footprint of food.

We supplement the emissions factors from 'The Big Climate Database' with more detailed emissions factors for seafood. These are sourced from the 'Seafood Carbon Emissions Tool' provided by Dalhousie University and the Monterey Bay Aquarium Seafood Watch® program.

NUTRITIONAL INFORMATION:

The calorie and macro-nutrient data are sourced from nutrition factors provided by WolframAlpha. These factors include calorie content and the mix of calories provided by protein, carbohydrates, saturated fat, and unsaturated fat.

FURTHER READING:

To explore more about the environmental and health impacts of food here are some references and resources:

Find out more, watch videos of all our recipes, or get in touch at www.climatechangekitchen.com

Find out more about climate change and net-zero at www.net-zero.blog

Read more about climate change in 'CLIMATE CHANGE and the road to NET-ZERO' by Mathew Hampshire-Waugh, https://net-zero.blog/the-book

Download 'The Big Climate Database' for free, and explore the life cycle emissions of more than 500 foods at https://denstoreklimadatabase.dk/en/download

Click through the 'Seafood Carbon Emissions Tool' to better understand the climate impact of seafood at http://seafoodco2.dal.ca

Browse 'Our World in Data' for an excellent background on food and climate change at https://ourworldindata.org/environmental-impacts-of-food

Learn more about low carbon food at the fork ranger https://www.forkranger.com

For more on healthy eating read Dietary Guidelines for Americans by the USDA or Government Dietary Recommendations by Public Health England.

DISCLAIMER

The information provided on the carbon footprint of food is dynamic and variable. The information provided in this book is a good estimate which can be used to provide general knowledge and guidance but cannot provide precise analysis of specific ingredients which require exacting data.

The nutritional information provided is based on generalized ingredients and is as such a good estimate. For a more accurate estimation of calories and macro-nutrient balance always refer to the nutritional labeling on the specific ingredients and food products you use. The information we provide is for general knowledge and you are responsible for all decisions pertaining to your health. Should you have any health concerns always consult a physician or health care professional.

Always use your best judgement when cooking with raw ingredients and seek expert advice if you are unsure. Take care not to injure yourself or others with knives, hot ovens, or other kitchen equipment. Please examine the contents of ingredients before the preparation and consumption of these recipes to ensure those eating the food are not allergic, intolerant, or adverse to any of the foodstuffs.

DEDICATION

Dedicated to GG who taught me how to cook, and to my amazing wife Charlotte and my incredible children Leonardo and Margot. I couldn't have finished this book without your love, support, and candid taste testing!

INDEX

TASTING NOTES
Aromatic 100, 108, 114, 116
Creamy 26, 36, 50, 54, 84, 96, 102, 104, 106, 132
Fresh 46, 56, 62, 86, 130
Nutty 60, 72, 92, 102, 132
Salty 56, 90, 92, 136, 140
Savory 48, 64, 90, 120, 140
Smoky 76, 82, 94, 110, 112, 128, 136
Sour 40, 90
Spicy 34, 64, 94, 108, 110, 112, 114, 116, 142
Sweet 20, 32, 50, 58, 66, 80, 98
Tangy 24, 42, 48, 80, 114, 122, 130

NUTRITIONAL LABELS
Balanced Macronutrients 14, 24, 26, 46, 66, 86, 92, 112, 120, 132
High Protein 22, 28, 48, 54, 64, 74, 128
Low Calorie 24, 34, 44, 46, 48, 56, 64, 66, 100, 108
Low Carbohydrate 30
Low Fat 28, 44, 78, 100, 108
Low Saturated Fat 24, 34, 44, 46, 48, 52, 66, 92, 100, 108, 112, 118
Vegan Option/Vegetarian 24, 34, 36, 38, 42, 46, 60, 78, 100, 108, 112, 120
Vegetarian 14, 18, 26, 32, 40, 56, 62, 66, 72, 86, 92

PERISHABLE INGREDIENTS
Anchovies 90
Apple 16, 60, 110
Asparagus 86
Aubergine 42, 92, 112
Avocado 20, 62, 76
Beans (butter) 52, 96
Beans (black or pinto) 78, 94
Beans (kidney) 94, 96
Beansprout 50, 142
Beet(root) 32, 58, 70, 94
Bell Pepper 20, 46, 76, 100, 108, 116, 118, 122, 124, 126, 130, 134
Bok Choy 48, 116

Bread (baguette) 24
Bread (bun) 16, 68, 70
Bread (flatbread) 128
Bread (loaf) 118
Breadcrumb 18, 26, 28, 30, 68, 70, 72, 80, 88, 96, 112
Broccoli (baby) 120, 126
Cabbage 16, 80, 130
Capers 90
Carrot 16, 18, 44, 66, 96, 100, 110, 120, 122, 124, 126, 142
Cashew Nut 14, 20, 36, 120
Cauliflower 34, 44, 108
Celery 44, 60, 96
Cheese (feta) 32, 56, 92
Cheese (hard) 26, 54, 72, 82, 84, 86, 88, 102, 132
Cheese (Mozzarella) 14, 62
Cheese (semi-hard) 20, 72
Chicken (breast or fillet) 20, 44, 50, 68, 76, 104, 106, 122, 124, 130, 134
Chicken (ground/mince) 30
Chicken (thigh) 22, 52, 74, 98, 114, 118, 128, 138
Chickpea 36, 52, 108
Chorizo 134
Clam 48, 134
Corn (baby) 116, 124
Corn (on the cob) 74
Courgette 18, 86, 116, 142
Cream 86, 98
Crème fraiche 60, 136
Cucumber 40, 46, 56
Egg 18, 26, 28, 32, 54, 58, 68, 80, 84, 102, 112, 136, 140, 142
Eggplant 42, 92, 112
Grape 60
Green bean 58
Jackfruit 16, 78
Leek 98
Lemon 36, 40, 42, 52, 54, 60, 80, 86, 92
Lettuce 56, 58, 64, 78, 128
Lime 38, 64, 66, 76, 116, 126
Macaroni 72

Mackerel 136
Mange Tout 66
Mayonnaise 54, 60
Milk (coconut) 50, 112, 114, 116
Milk (oat) 44, 50, 102
Milk (soy) 44, 50
Mushroom 18, 120
Mushroom (shiitake) 120
Mussels 48
Noodle (egg/wheat) 44, 120, 130
Noodle (rice) 50, 126
Noodles (Udon/ramen) 140
Olives 14, 56, 58, 90
Pancetta 82, 94
Papaya 66
Parsnip 100
Pastry (puff) 18
Peas 38, 86, 132, 134, 136
Pork (belly) 140, 142
Pork (ground/mince) 70, 82, 94, 102
Pork (loin) 80, 110
Potato 26, 28, 74, 110, 128
Ricotta 86
Sausage 96
Scallop 126, 132
Sour Cream 14, 94
Sweet potato 14, 20, 32, 78, 100, 116, 118
Tahini 42
Tamarind Paste 126
Tomato 14, 24, 46, 52, 56, 62, 76, 104, 118, 128
Tomato (canned) 82, 88, 90, 92, 94, 96, 102, 108
Tomato (cherry) 38, 58, 64, 66
Tortilla (wrap) 20, 76
Tuna (canned) 28, 58, 88
Tuna (fresh) 64
Yogurt (coconut) 106, 108
Yogurt (plain) 40, 54, 60, 76, 104, 138
Yogurt (soy) 54, 138
Zucchini 18, 86, 116, 142

Printed in Great Britain
by Amazon